Endorsements

In *Holy Plot Twists*, Amanda Schaefer masterfully guides you through the sacred journey of discovering God's fingerprints in your life story. With raw honesty and tender insight, she shares her path from childhood trauma to transformative faith, while offering a practical framework for readers to uncover their own holy moments. This isn't just another Christian memoir—it's an invitation to see how God has been writing your story all along, even in the chapters you'd rather forget. Through carefully crafted questions and gentle guidance honed during her years as a podcaster interviewing others about their faith journeys, Amanda helps you transform your painful past into purpose. For anyone wondering if God can redeem their broken places, this book offers hope and a practical path forward.

— Lori Ann Wood, author of *Divine Detour: The Path You'd Never Choose Can Lead to the Faith You've Always Wanted*

———o-o-o———

Amanda Schaefer shares her heart and her journey to faith in her new book, *Holy Plot Twists*. I met Amanda on her podcast, *A Cup of Gratitude*, and we instantly bonded as friends and fellow sojourners through this life with all its ups and downs, challenges and victories, and yes, those unexpected, sometimes terrorizing, usually beneficial, and amazing plot twists! Her new book also encourages us to journal our own life's many twists and turns. We might be surprised to see how the hardest plot twists were the best ones for us!

— Martha Bolton, playwright and Emmy-nominated writer and the author of 89 books, including *Bob Hope's Wartime Correspondence with the GIs of World War II*, *Josiah for President*, and *The Rise and Fall of Miss Fannie's Biscuits* (co-authored with Wanda Brunstetter)

In Holy Plot Twists, Amanda Schaefer captures how God weaves through the chapters of our lives—even when the plot takes unexpected turns. Amanda's warm and authentic voice makes Holy Plot Twists a treasure for anyone seeking encouragement and renewed faith. Whether at the beginning of your journey, navigating a challenging season, or celebrating God's goodness, Holy Plot Twists will remind you that God is the author of your story, and it is still being written.

— Mary Rooney Armand, creator of ButterflyLiving.org and author of *Understanding Your Identity in Christ* and *Life Changing Stories.*

———o-o-o———

God has a way of faithfully directing the course of our lives, even when we don't recognize it. In *Holy Plot Twists*, Amanda Schaefer does a beautiful job pointing us toward the ever-present love and care of our Creator for every chapter of our story. With thought-provoking questions, an empathetic voice and a compassionately wise heart, Amanda invites us to lay our painful past at the feet of Jesus, and in return, we will see Him write redemption and restoration into our present and future. Everyone would benefit from this healing book!"

— Becky Beresford - speaker, coach & author of *She Believed HE Could, So She Did*

———o-o-o———

Anyone listening to Amanda Schaefer's well-loved (and wildly successful) podcast knows she's the real deal: authentic, humble, broken—and vibrantly transformed by the living Christ. Now, in this candid and brave account, she shares how Jesus entered her dark backstory and how he's rewriting her life. *Holy Plot Twists* is no simple memoir, however. Through probing questions like those in her interviews, she calls readers to bring their own stories into God's light for healing and hope—and infuses us with the courage to do exactly that.

— Cheryl Grey Bostrom, award-winning author of *Sugar Birds* and *Leaning on Air*

I first met Amanda Schaefer when we were collaborating together on a writing project with several other women. I was immediately drawn to her warmth and sincere love for God and for people. When I started listening to her podcast, *A Cup of Gratitude*, I was hooked. Amanda has a genuine gift for making her guests feel safe to open up and tell their deepest stories. Within the pages of *Holy Plot Twists*, Amanda shares this gift once again by inviting her readers on a journey into the deeply intimate story of God's grace in her life while cultivating an environment where we can reflect and do the same. Just as she does in her interviews, Amanda asks the questions that cause us to contemplate the holy plot twists in our lives, those places where God reveals Himself to us in unexpected and glorious ways. I am grateful to know Amanda personally and to have experienced firsthand the amazing gift she has of making each and every person she meets feel like family, as she encourages us to share our stories for God's glory.

— Dawn R. Ward, author of *From Guilt to Grace: Hope and Healing for Christian Moms of Addicted Children* and founder of The Faith to Flourish

HOLY
PLOT
TWISTS

GOD IS STILL WRITING YOUR STORY

AMANDA SCHAEFER

Published by Abundance Books, LLC
Kalamazoo, MI
abundance-books.com

Cover image by Marco Montalti - Italy, September 21, 2020, Stock file ID 1280370725 collection essentials
Cover Design by Amanda Schaefer and Jackson Schaefer
Interior Design by Taryn Golliher

10 9 8 7 6 5 4 3 2 1

Contents

Dedication

· O ·

I dedicate this book to God and to the family he gave me. I am grateful for every page of the story written in my life. Although there were chapters never intended for me to endure, the transformative power of God's love has made them beautiful and purposeful. Looking back, I can see God's presence and compassion in even the darkest days.

To my mom, who would have been so proud to read this book, we miss and love you dearly. Please tell Jesus we say hello. To my dad, your love and support have been a constant source of strength. To my amazing daughter, Lauren, and my equally fantastic son, Jackson, your help with these pages has been invaluable. I thank God every day for who you have grown up to be. I will never be able to fully express the profound impact your lives have had on mine. Thank you for always loving me so well.

Introduction

The person I was before meeting Jesus is not who I am now. His love changed me. In part one of this book, I share my story to highlight the impact he has had in my life. I talk about parts of my life I never have before to show you how God worked in my broken places.

In part two, you will find an interactive journal created just for you. As you answer pivotal questions and spend time looking back through your life with God, you will be blessed by your own story. My years of experience as a podcast host have helped me develop this format that will unlock your past by highlighting significant themes and threads in your life to better understand your authentic self.

Be astonished at every twist and turn. Experience healing, embrace forgiveness, and discover purpose. You will see your life from an entirely new perspective.

By asking my podcast guests to share their stories starting in their childhood, I began to see a pattern emerge. This practice of looking back with God revealed a deeper sense of purpose and gave new insight to all. Hearing from the One who created you is a powerful experience.

I can't interview everyone, but I felt God asking me to share what I had learned with as many people as possible. That is why I wrote this book for you. Think of this as your prerecording conversation with me. And if you want to share your story on my podcast after you are done, feel free to contact me.

I invite you to turn the page. Invest in yourself. You are worth it!

Before I share my story with you, we will look at the heart of God together to understand how he loves us differently. Every detail about you matters to him. He has made you uniquely. Even your fingerprints are an important part of your story.

Let's look at how God allows us to cocreate with him. Do you know how your fingerprints were formed? I didn't. Join me in chapter one for a glimpse of the amazing details that tell us about the heart of the God who created us.

Chapter One

Fingerprints

Question: Do you think God is your Creator?

————o-o-o————

Our stories are as unique as our fingerprints. God created each of us differently. Look around and consider the variation of God's creation.

No two sets of fingerprints are the same. This made me curious, so I went looking for answers. I am surprised it was not taught in my biology class. I wonder why it isn't preached from a pulpit. As I pondered my own uniqueness, God revealed a truth that transformed my life.

Psalm 139:13–14 (ESV) says, "I am fearfully and wonderfully made." God has designed us down to the tiniest detail. But what I found when I studied the science behind the formation of our fingerprints is that God allows us to be cocreators with him. In a beautiful dance deep inside a mother's womb as her baby forms, so does this alliance with God. When a baby is seventeen weeks old, halfway through a normal pregnancy, fingerprints become set. God allows choice before we are even born, declaring a baby a person with cognitive free will and identity.

As the baby forms, the pads on their fingers and toes are tiny blank slates. At the same time the baby has enough muscle, bone, and brain function to reach out to touch its surroundings, its fingers and toes are being subjected to pressure from the fluid around them. The soft developing skin bends and wrinkles. This is when our fingerprints form because of choice, will, thought, and action. Each time a baby touches its surroundings, ridges, arches, loops, and whorls form.

Every child reaches out differently, just as every person is made uniquely. The fingerprints are a result of working together with our Creator. God gives the baby the ability to reach and a brain to direct its arm outward. He gives the child free will to decide when to reach out.

Hidden deep within the untouched microcosm of a mother's womb, we see the creation and the Creator working together, unified for the first of many times to come.

We are identifiable by the world we are born into because of the first ways we choose to reach out to it. Our identity is formed by connecting with our surroundings.

Spiritually this happens in our hearts as well. When we reach out to Jesus, our hearts form their imprints. In Christ, our hearts are transformed too. We are brought back into the garden to be who God originally intended for us to be. Jesus covers us and our spiritual life is restored.

God didn't just make a bunch of little gods. He created sons and daughters. He cares about you as a loving parent, and he goes to great lengths to show it. No detail is too small for God; he joins us in every ridge and whorl.

The fingerprints you leave in the world leave traces of you. Your heart, in turn, leaves imprints of God. We leave fingerprints everywhere, on everything. Even now, by touching these pages, you leave a trace of yourself.

Can you imagine what the world would look like if we could see our fingerprints? What if we could see all the fingerprints on everything around us over time? Can you imagine if each set were a different color to represent its unique origin? The echoes of our interactions and human experiences are just sitting there, written all over us like tattoos for all to see.

Our stories leave imprints on those they touch. We are writing with invisible ink on the lives we intersect with.

The ultimate fingerprint of God on our life is the blood of Jesus, which covers us when we accept our need for salvation.

The blood restores our identity and brings us back into the family. God marks us with his spiritual fingerprint. He seals us with the mark of his Holy Spirit.

In the family of God, we get to walk with God. We get to choose if we want to be with him or not. We interact with one another and the world around us, reaching out when and how we choose. It's a big world full of tiny details as small as the ridges and whorls of our fingerprints.

Look at your hands. Those fingerprints you see formed when you reached out with your own free will as a baby. You wanted to connect because you were created to connect. God made family.

God is a Father who cherishes you. His mighty arms long to hold your tiny frame close. "Lay upon my chest, child," he beckons in a rich and comforting tone. "Rest your weary head on me. I will keep you safe." He nuzzles you close to his chin as he sings over you with rejoicing.

The God whose voice boomed into the silent nothing like mighty rushing waters, the One who created everything, whispers to you, his cherished child. A Father whose mere breath could twist the heavy boughs of cedars, his holy presence shattering them into smithereens, purposefully quiets his voice to speak sweetly to you.

As he holds you tenderly, waiting for you to settle into his chest, his heartbeat quiets your breathing and brings you to a place of peace. God's eternal lullaby circles around you as his hopes and dreams for your future begin to show radiantly on his face. A smile only you can bring to his heart fills him and he calls you his own.

Like every good father, he is ready to catch you when you fall, bending low to soften the ground beneath your tottering feet. He softly covers you with his holy robes, praying blessings over your life. God is in this for the love and nothing more. You are the apple of his eye.

This Fatherly love fills his thoughts as he becomes expectant, knowing the joy you will have from being a creator too. We are made in his image, with the ability to leave our mark on the world around us. God has a plan for your life and a calling for all of who you are.

It all begins with Jesus. He was willing to be contained inside a mother's womb, growing as a fragile baby.

Can you imagine all the places where Jesus' fingerprints touched the world he created? The Bible tells us stories about when Jesus wrote with his finger in the sand, the blind eyes he healed with his touch, and the carpentry tools he learned to work with. Consider the hugs he gave those he loved and the hands he held. Think about the plate he passed to the one who betrayed him and the cup he drank from. Amazingly, they were on the cross he had to carry. His fingerprints were on all those things, and now he, himself, is the fingerprint of God, placed on each of us by his holy blood shed on the cross. When God looks at us, he sees Jesus.

Sharing the unique perspective God has gifted you with is imperative. You will be able to fully share it once you fully understand it. God started writing your story when you were still in your mother's womb.

When you take the time to go back and look at your life, intentionally seeking the moments God was working, you will find an intricate and breathtaking story.

Having considered God's attention to detail, do you think God can do more than you might be able to imagine? Holy plot twists are those times where God can do what we thought was impossible. Before we jump into my story, I want us to consider together how and why God intervenes with these holy plot twists to better understand God's perspective of our stories.

Chapter Two
Holy Plot Twists

—————— • O • ——————

Question: Do you think God can do the impossible?

——————o-o-o——————

Holy plot twists are those times when everything looks one way, and God flips it around, making it completely different. It is important to know how God thinks and works in our lives to fully grasp his ability to transform situations.

All our stories begin in the garden. God formed Adam from the dust and breathed his Spirit into him. God took Eve from Adam's side. He gave them everything they needed. The only thing he asked them not to do was the thing they could not resist doing. Sounds like a typical Father-child relationship, right? Unfortunately, the repercussions of their disobedience meant death. A spiritual disconnection from the holy God who created them to be his family. One bite of fruit changed their lives forever.

Our lives are affected by the events in the garden. We are born into the world sinful and spiritually dead. But God did not leave us that way. He had a plan to bring his children back to himself. God's love for us was so great that he sent Jesus to bring us home.

The most challenging aspects of your life in God's hands can serve a greater, more profound purpose. A shift in perspective can change your understanding of your own story. Perhaps, like me, you have missed what God was doing at certain times. Sometimes we are so focused on our circumstances we can't see how God could transform them. To better understand how God works, let's look at the story of Joseph in the Bible.

God gave Joseph a dream. But after he shared that dream with his family, his brothers threw him into a pit. His family did not understand his dream from God.

Joseph's brothers sold him into captivity, but God continued to give Joseph favor wherever he ended up. People against him tried to keep him from doing what God had prepared for him. Eventually, he ended up in jail. In that prison cell, he still had God's favor. Joseph was able to interpret the dreams of the prisoners.

When Pharaoh had a dream that needed interpretation, the cupbearer remembered Joseph. The guards brought him out of his prison cell, and Joseph rose to the position depicted in his vision given years before.

At first glance, his life appeared to be unfair. Do you think prison was the best place for Joseph? He was lied to, rejected, lied about, and forgotten. What if God kept Joseph in position for his plan? Joseph saved hundreds of thousands of people and restored his relationship with his family from the position God placed him.

At the end of the story, Joseph tells his brothers this truth: "You meant evil against me, but God meant it for good, to bring about that many people should be kept alive, as they are today" (Genesis 50:20 ESV). This is a perfect example of a holy plot twist.

In this book, you will discover the holy plot twists in your life. You will uncover the moments you may have missed because you were so busy living life. Perhaps, like Joseph, you were so focused on the bars, the pit, the lies, or the rejection that you missed what God was doing.

God created you with a purpose, talents, and passions. We live in a sinful world, so we also experience trauma and brokenness. But God uses it all. He does not waste a thing. He will take the very thing that seems like the end and instead make it your clarion call.

God's ways and thinking are above ours. He can use even the

most shattered pieces, the sharpest moments, those things we don't even want to look at or remember.

God can bring the best out of any situation.

As a podcast host, I have had the incredible opportunity to hear the stories of God's children. Through those interviews, I've seen how God works in the lives of his people in the most unexpected ways.

Many people didn't know God until after they'd already lived through hard stories. I was one of them. What I have learned since is that in the waiting, in the suffering, in the trauma, in the rejection, in the loneliness, in the chaos, we were never alone.

The purpose of this book is to use the talents and experiences that God has given me to help you discover the treasures in your testimony.

I wrote this book to help you understand your whole story so you can see the beautiful threads of Jesus working in your life. The best way to do that is to start at the beginning. Together, we will start in your childhood and work up to the present.

I remember when I first felt God ask me to start a blog. Knowing nothing about how to do it made my throat dry and my hands shake. God asked me to be vulnerable, and that was something I had never been completely. "What if people don't want to be around me after I share what I am going through?" I said aloud, looking towards the ceiling as I spoke and imagining my voice breaking through it to ascend before God's throne. My chin began to quiver, and my voice cracked sharply as the tears fell fast and wild on my face. I asked God for another way to serve him.

"Do not be afraid, I am with you," God replied. I felt his presence envelop me right there in the room. I reached down to take off my shoes, throwing them across the floor, and fell to my knees. Slumped over with my forehead touching the rough wide-plank wooden floor, I cried until I was empty of tears. God began to do something miraculous in that moment. I could feel it. A fresh anointing of his Holy Spirit fell, filling my heart from the inside out with his peace and purpose. God was with me; there was no denying it.

Instead of being afraid because you don't know the next step, what if your first thought was that God knows what comes next?

We don't have to worry about the rest of the plan because he's got it and has it in a way we never could. God is good, and he knows the whole story. He cares about what is best for us!

In God's plan, even when we chose to disobey, he would not leave us there alone. He sent his Son Jesus to twist our fate. Sin entered the world in the Garden of Eden, and the guards took Jesus from the Garden of Gethsemane. Sin entered through the fruit of a tree, and Jesus took upon himself our sin nailed to a tree for our transgressions. Sin brought thorns and pain to the earth as part of its curse, and Jesus bore a crown of thorns and endured pain on the cross to break the curse the only way possible, through the shedding of his perfect blood. He made all things new. Jesus restored us to a relationship with a holy God.

God reconciled us back to himself. God loves you. Jesus went to the cross for you. God is the God of holy plot twists.

Your next chapter awaits its beginning. No matter what your circumstances, another sentence is being written. Let God transform your "right now" and help you see its eternal purpose. Are you ready to hear my story? I remember always feeling anxious and afraid. Looking back, I think it all started when my mom told me our house was haunted.

Chapter Three

Going Home

—————— ·o-o-o· ——————

Question: Do you ever remember praying or talking to God, being angry at God, or any interaction that started with you?

——————o-o-o——————

I was only four years old. I ran upstairs and threw myself on my bed face down. I began to cry. My hands were shaking, and my stomach felt like it was being twisted like a wet rag. I found the strength to sit up and reach my tiny arms around my belly to hug myself. The flannel pajamas I was wearing felt buttery soft, and for a moment, I forgot why I was there. But then I remembered. Beginning to rock back and forth on my bed, I finally talked to the ghosts. I had never seen them, but my family had told me enough stories at the breakfast table to convince me they were real.

"Don't show yourself to me," I yelled, surprising myself as my voice broke into the silence. My words floated around me, eventually falling to the ground and disappearing into the worn olive-green carpet. Shivering at the thought of seeing a ghost, I curled myself into the fetal position and pulled my blanket over my head. When I opened my eyes, I could see the tiny strawberries with smiling faces that peppered the pattern covering me. Seeing these familiar friends made me exhale the breath I had not even realized I was still holding. If I could stay under here forever, I thought, everything would be okay.

"Amanda, come down here, please," I heard my mom yell up the stairs. I didn't want to leave the safety of that moment. Slowly lifting the covers from my head and gently placing them back on the bed, I sat up and readied myself to put my feet back on the floor. I was shaking again. It was at that moment any bit of an understanding of God being real or good left me. I didn't know God. I only knew about him. People had told me he protected us, but I imagined him so far off because he wasn't there to help me. He must be a mean old man who was too busy for my little problems. That was a pivotal moment. I believed God was not for me or with me, and my fear was confirmed. Those ghosts were real.

The next night, I woke up to go to the bathroom, and at the end of my bed was a giant shadowy figure with arms crossed looking off to the side. But when I opened my eyes, it was as if it knew I was awake. It turned its head slowly towards me, holding its clawlike hands before its chest. I trembled at the sight of it staring at me and pulled my arms together in front of me as if I could protect myself. Then I couldn't move. I was frozen in place. It began to fall towards me with its hands out, ready to grab me. I threw the covers up over my head in horror, shaking, and the sweat on my forehead started to drip into my eyes, stinging them. I lay there waiting for the weight of this horrific monster to land on top of me, screaming at the top of my lungs in my mind but not daring to utter a word aloud.

I don't know how long it was; it felt like hours, but eventually, I got the courage to peek out from under the covers. Nothing was there. Now, when I look back, I believe this was demonic. When I told the story to my family, my mom said it was probably a ghost, just another layer to the lie.

I wonder if I was looking for these things because I thought ghosts were real or if I was given a glimpse behind the curtain into the supernatural world around me.

Trying to go back and remember my childhood gets more difficult every year, not because I'm old and having trouble remembering but because I'm new. I'm reborn in Christ.

I liken it to those of us with children who are trying to remember what we were like before we had them. It's a two-dimensional thing we can only partially recall; we are transformed. We're suddenly mothers, and it's part of our new identity, so we can't fully remember the feelings of who we were before.

I have some fond memories from my childhood but also some troublesome and traumatic ones too. I was the youngest of three children, seven years younger than my sister and five years younger than my brother, who has special needs.

When I was little, doctors told my parents they thought I had leukemia. I don't have much personal memory of this. I have heard stories of being held down by my mom while they took the bone marrow test and of my bloodcurdling screams.

I do, however, remember going for weekly blood checkups. The first time I went, I sat nervously on a metal stool beside the nurse, who smiled at me kindly. "Now remember," she said, leaning in to touch my shoulder gently, "You get a lollipop if you sit still, okay sweetie?"

"Yes, ma'am." I wished she would offer me a Hershey bar instead.

The needle was short but sharp. It made me want to cry out when she pushed it down into my finger. A ruby-red drop of blood bubbled up onto my fingertip. "Now I am going to put the blood on the slide, honey," the nurse said, grasping my hand. "This part won't hurt." She pressed the blood onto the little rectangular piece of glass. The nurse took another slide and placed it on top of the first before carefully laying them both on the metal table next to her. The table was covered with a white fabric, and I wondered why. "That's it, sweetie. Wonderful job!" She stood up to guide me out of the room. I got used to this weekly routine and figured that everyone had that experience until, one day while talking to a friend, I realized that I was different.

When I asked my parents about it, they told me they thought I was very sick. My white blood count was off, so they had been convinced I was going to have leukemia. I never did, and here I am, sixty, writing to you.

My mom was prone to anxiety. Dealing with my brother and his special needs and then thinking that I was sick was traumatic for her. I think it changed her brain chemistry.

When my parents first married, my mom graduated from college early; she was at the top of her class. When they moved for my dad's job, she got bored and went into a low-income neighborhood, where she got a job as a teacher but didn't tell my dad. He felt suspicious and followed her one day. When he saw where she was working, he told her she couldn't stay there. That day, my mother listened to my father and lost some of her boldness.

That was the beginning of my mom losing her confidence. While growing up, her mother had some emotional difficulties, and my mom had to do a lot of things around the house and lost out on some of her childhood.

My dad started traveling for work. He went to South America, Riyadh, and other far-off places for his job. I remember him bringing me dolls from everywhere he went, and I had a vast collection.

When my dad went away, my mom got even more fearful. Some of my earliest memories are of my mom crying and coming to me, a little girl, for advice and comfort. "Amanda, your sister is upsetting me, and your dad is away, so I don't know what to do. Do you think I am doing the right thing punishing her?"

"I guess so," I said, wanting to comfort her. Mom had been crying again, and I wanted her to be happy. She started to sob softly. I was barely five years old. I didn't understand what was happening, but my heart wanted everyone to be okay. "I think you did a great job, Mom," I said, hoping these words would calm my mother down.

My mother reached forward and hugged me tightly. Her affection made me feel like I had answered the right way. "Thank you, sweetheart," she said, her warm tears pressed against my shoulder.

My mom was drinking from a wine glass. I noticed she did that a lot when Dad was away. Now, when I look back, I know that I should have been playing or watching a TV show or reading a book, not consoling an adult, but I didn't know any better. Even more importantly, as time passed, I learned to cater to my mom's emotions, which sometimes meant not feeling or expressing my own. My mother had always been sensitive, and I had a compassionate little heart. The direction of love and care in a family is supposed to go from parent to child, not from child to parent. It was moments like this when parental inversion began to turn my life upside down and inside out.

My older sister was so much older I felt like a bother to her, and my older brother, because he had special needs, seemed to go from being older to equal to younger than me as our childhood progressed. I took on a motherly role with him as well.

I remember one time when he was planning to run away from home. As soon as he told me, I knew I had to help him. "What if I go with you?"

"Okay, "he answered. "But I am ready now, so hurry up!"

"What are you bringing with you?" I asked him quietly.

"Just this bag." He showed me a little suitcase he had packed all by himself.

"Okay, I will pack a bag too." Once I was done, we put on our coats and hats simultaneously.

"Shhhh," he said, pulling on his boots. "I don't want Mom to hear us."

"Okay, I will be quiet," I whispered as I tied my little red leather shoes.

We headed out the front door together, crossing the front lawn. Up ahead was a small footbridge to cross over the top of our creek. On the other side was a church and a little schoolhouse. As we neared the bridge, I instinctively started to ask my brother questions to reroute him back home again. He loved to eat, so I said, "Hey, Doug, I wonder what mom is making for dinner tonight?"

He stopped for a minute and put down his suitcase to adjust the hand-knit beanie on top of his head. He pulled it down over his ears as the crisp air swirled around us, picking up the brown, crunchy leaves from the ground. He grabbed the handle of his suitcase in his right hand and trudged ahead. "I don't know, but I am getting hungry."

"I am starving," I blurted out. "I bet we are having meatloaf and baked potatoes." I knew this was his favorite meal.

"Wow, that would taste good," he said, stopping to think.

"And what do you think we would have for dessert?" I asked, baiting him even further.

"Apple pie," he said, licking his lips.

"I am thirsty," I said. "Did you bring any water?"

He stopped and pulled out his Cub Scout canteen, surprising me that he had brought some. "Here you go," he said, smiling quite proudly.

I turned open the cap from the canteen and raised it to my lips. The water was cool and crisp. "Mmmmm, that's good." I twisted the cap back on and threw the strap over my shoulder.

"Hey, that's mine!"

"I didn't bring any," I said sadly, handing him back the water.

"Maybe we should head back home," he said. "You are thirsty, and I am hungry, and after all, mom will have way too much food left over if we don't go back. It might go bad."

"Great idea." We turned back, never having even made it off our property. "Doug, thanks for taking care of me." I had not realized that here, too, I was more concerned about his well-being than a younger sister should be. I had stepped into another role that was not meant for me.

Instinctively, I took on the role of mothering him, always explaining and helping him with things. I had lost the most carefree childhood moments between that and the parental inversion I experienced.

I have vivid memories of being afraid for no real reason. One night when my parents were out and left me with a babysitter, something fell and made a thunderous noise. Even though it was only something falling, my fear froze me in place. My heart raced at the thought of what sinister character could have broken in. I remember feeling frightened at the idea that a ghost could have knocked a picture from the wall. None of these things were real, but fear makes us believe lies.

After that, I remember being afraid whenever I was alone. I grew up in a farmhouse built in the seventeenth century. Around the time I was four or five years old, my mom told us stories at the table about the ghosts who lived with us. She talked about poltergeists and objects being in one place and suddenly being in another.

I also remember having a Ouija board in the house. We discussed UFOs regularly and even looked for them in the night sky. I believed. These things were real to me. The enemy had already set these lies like concrete hardened in my soul.

During this same time, I experienced sexual abuse, which happened outside of our home. I don't remember clearly all the details of those events, but I cannot forget the migraine headaches that plagued me right after the abuse began. I never told anyone about it until I was grown up. I pushed down the feelings and the trauma, and I became anxious too.

There was so much happening inside of me, and I had nowhere to go with it and no one to talk to. I just kept pushing it down and pushing it down. My heart was like a trash compactor. One day, I knew I was going to explode.

More days than not, I lay on my bed, my head throbbing. Tiny undulating circles danced before my eyes.

"I can't see," I said, frightened by the blurry world around me. My mom offered to get a washcloth for my eyes, leaving me in the dark and quiet room. I didn't understand at the time, but I was having an ocular migraine.

Outside, it was bright and sunny. I had been playing happily in the woods next to our home when my eyesight began to blur. As I walked to the house, I started to feel the pain deep inside my head, right behind my eyes. "Mom, I feel sick," I said, holding my temples.

"Go upstairs and lie down," my mom said.

As I climbed up the back stairs, each creak in the risers beneath my shuffling feet made me wince in pain. While other kids were outside playing, I lay still and silent with a cool washcloth over my eyes. Trailing off to sleep was the only real relief I could get. The aspirin my mom gave me made me feel queasy.

I woke up at dinner time. Another day was completely gone. This was my new normal.

Growing up, I was so busy trying to live up to the standards of the conditional love that enveloped our home dynamics that I got lost. I desperately tried to fit into the "Norman Rockwell" family image my mom felt she needed to perpetuate. I had no idea who I was supposed to be.

Over the years, I went from being a vibrant little girl who told stories, wrote books, and put on endless plays, to being a reticent, shy, insular, anxious, and depressed teen.

I have this one great memory; I don't want to give you the impression that I don't have good memories. When I look back, the bad memories are indicators of what was happening to me and the lies that I believed about who I was.

My parents were so supportive and fostered my creativity. My mother taught me to make scrambled eggs; I was only four years old. I don't know if we teach kids that early these days, but I was capable. She explained it all so I could do it on my own. Cooking by myself made me feel confident, and I loved it.

As I got more comfortable cooking, I started wanting to make my parents breakfast on the weekends. One day, I discovered the spice cabinet. I rummaged through it, searching for treasure and gleefully shaking the unknown spices into the eggs. Sometimes, I'd add cheese or some sort of vegetable, but always lots and lots of spice.

As a toddler chef, I carefully carried my offerings to my parents' room, excited they would try my newest creation. I brought them breakfast in bed every Saturday morning. They thanked me and smiled, but apparently, I wouldn't leave. I stood there happily, watching them eat my masterpiece. They always told me how wonderful it was. That buoyed me up.

They waited until I was older to tell me the truth so it wouldn't hinder or hurt me. They told me those concoctions were disgusting. Mom said it was tough to swallow them, but they did not want to squelch my creativity. I am very thankful. To this day, I love to cook and experiment, and I'm so glad for that part of who I am.

When I performed my plays, mom and dad always watched them. When I wrote my books, they read them with enthusiasm.

My mom was an English teacher. She shared my love for writing. Mom was good at encouraging me to be creative, and I am eternally indebted for that.

Looking back and knowing that God created me and deposited these things in me on purpose is thrilling. I want to thank God for making me creative and allowing me to see beauty and purpose in everyday life. This attribute has become my superpower. I am so thankful to be able to express myself through things I write, draw, and make; it is incredible.

Unfortunately, as time went on, I went through many stages. I made my way into junior high and high school. I started smoking, I started drinking, I started experimenting with drugs, and eventually I became promiscuous too. I did not reveal any of these things to my family. I am unsure how I got away with most things when I look back. I am amazed at how God protected me! I was desperately trying not to feel anything. I did so many dangerous things that I should not still be alive. There were so many times disastrous things could have happened to me or should have happened to me, yet here I am.

Those times taught me what it is like to walk through life feeling numb. I know people who don't want to feel their feelings. I can appreciate that firsthand. Trauma recognizes trauma. I have a deep empathy for others in pain.

I could best describe my parents' relationship as codependent. I did not know what that was back then; I thought that is what a healthy marriage looked like. They had some beautiful things about their relationship; each had some excellent characteristics. My parents have read everything I have written about my past. Because of this, we have discussed things that needed processing, and I have seen them trying to understand my point of view for what felt like the first time. It was endearing and healing, like a salve to my angry wounds.

I made my way to college, where I continued making horrible decisions. I came home again and eventually found myself married with a child on the way. I had no idea how to be a parent.

I had my first child and experienced unconditional love

for the first time. I was still lost, anxious, and depressed. I hadn't dealt with what had happened to me, but my love for my daughter was inexplicable and probably the purest thing about me.

Her dad and I didn't know what we were doing. We were too immature to have a child. Eventually, I found myself feeling unfulfilled, and I divorced my first husband. I made an earnest effort to stay close and did my best to keep some sort of relationship.

I got married again, and nine years later, I had my second child, my son, but I still didn't know Jesus. I was so dysfunctional. But being a mom was where I came alive. I loved my kids with everything I had; I would have done anything for them, and this love was where God first showed me how he felt about me.

It is crucial to see who I was before I met Jesus, what I had been through, and what events shaped me. I didn't ever think about Jesus. He was just another character in a book I hadn't read. I even got to a point where I made fun of Christians and Christianity. I stopped attending church and had tuned out paying attention years before. My parents took me to church every week throughout my childhood, but I never remember wanting to attend. Going to a building on Sunday mornings where they talked about things I didn't understand and wasn't interested in felt like a chore.

God didn't seem real. He was a far-off, mean old man, the one I knew as a preschooler who did not care about me. I wanted nothing to do with him.

God made me one way, and life spoke over me another. The actions and reactions of people had muddied the clear living water meant to flow through me. Anxiety, depression, and emotional and physical trauma created a foundation in me constructed with lies. I thought this was who I was and how my life had to be.

I waded through the thick mire of my everyday life with no hope, just trying to get to the point where I could sleep at night. The only positive things were my children. I think I was only my true self with them. I would allow myself to be creative when we played because I was trying to show them how to be something I no longer was.

It's how I started; it's what God intended for me. God didn't give up on me. He continued to pursue me. God was with me; I just could not see past the anxiety and the fear. I had built up an impenetrable wall around me. God never gave up pursuing me, but I did not understand that until I finally heard Jesus' voice.

One of the most beautiful things God did was allow me to be a mother, even amid two marriages that he did not consecrate. I never even asked for his advice. As I raised my children, I experienced unconditional love. When I was with them, I experienced the lightness, joy, peace, and creativity that I could have had as a child. God began to restore me little by little through motherhood, giving me back those pieces of my childhood the world had stolen from me. He made me whole again.

I believe God used my children to begin cracking open the hardened shell that had become my heart. It was from the place of being a mom that I began to believe that someone could love me like that. Because of the sharp, broken fissures, I could finally hear Jesus. He had been pursuing me all along, telling me from the beginning that he loved me. I believed him. The little child living inside of me was ready for an excellent, perfect Daddy to love, encourage, and protect her.

Although my heart was ready, I didn't know a thing about the spiritual battles I would face when I chose Jesus. I had never heard about the enemy of my soul. I didn't know he was anything more than a cartoon character until he attacked me ferociously. He was stealthy and relentless, never wanting me to know the true love God had for me. He wanted to destroy me!

Chapter Four

Lost and Found

— • ○ • —

Question: Have you ever been the only one to see a situation from a different perspective?

————o-o-o————

When I closed my eyes, I saw disturbing things. I began having thoughts that I knew I wasn't thinking, horrible thoughts about God. I can't even use those words here. They make me wince and shiver to recall. "F*** God. F*** him!"

"No, that's not what I think." I shouted at my bedroom walls and quickly turned to pace the floor again. It felt like I was wearing a path into the tan shag carpet beneath me.

"Dear God, I don't know how to pray right now. Help me! I don't know what's happening to me!" My chin quivered as I tried to speak. I fell to my knees right in front of my bed. The comforter looked strangely bright in the morning sunlight. So bright it made me squint.

I pressed my hands against my ears to try to keep the curses out, but they just kept coming like fiery darts, one after another, piercing through me. Over and over. "F*** God! F*** God! F*** him!" I felt nauseous and bent over, clutching my stomach with my hands. The hot tears falling from my eyes stung as they left me.

"Am I going crazy?" I shouted so loud that my dog ran scampering out of the room, thinking I was yelling at her. "Bucky, come back," I whispered, reaching my hand out to her in vain. "Help me, God, please help me," I muttered with my face planted firmly in my hands. Tears fell on the rug beneath me, and as I watched them drop, I wondered if this torture would ever end.

When I dared close my eyes, I saw a man's face. His pale skin was almost translucent, and he had no hair. The way he looked at me was menacing, mocking me as the corners of his mouth began to turn up to form a smirk. I quickly opened my eyes and then closed them again. He was still there, looking right at me, not blinking, not even once. Without a word, he made my body quake. My hands shook as I lifted them to cry out to God again. I could hear my heartbeat in my ears. It was deafening.

Somehow, I knew that it was this man whose voice I had heard cursing God. I sensed he had been trying to fool me into thinking the voice was my own. "God, I don't know much about talking to you, but I know that you can do anything, so please, can you do something about me seeing and hearing these things? Would you have your angels pull a stone slab across my mind to keep out these thoughts and images?" I prayed a few times and wondered why I asked for a stone slab. "This little light of mine, I'm going to let it shine," I sang softly. I did not know why I was singing. It was something instinctual. But I could feel it refocusing me and bringing me peace. I took a deep breath in through my nostrils and let it out slowly through my lips. I am not sure why, but it felt as if singing the song kept the attack at bay. "God, was that you, are you answering my prayer?" I wondered aloud. In my heart, the answer was yes.

These attacks continued for weeks. Singing was the only way they would stop. My parents were Christians, but they didn't seem to notice what I was going through. It was not until I finally told everyone I had accepted Jesus that I could talk about these darker things, and even then, no one knew what I was talking about.

It was just God and me. As I continued to trust him, God quenched every fiery dart. The man stopped appearing, and the voices were silenced.

I had a dream one night, more like a nightmare. In the dream, I was in my bed in the same room I was sleeping in. My dog Bucky woke me up because she heard something. As Bucky's lips curled to show her teeth, I listened to her snarl. I got off the bed and went to the doorway to look down the hallway with her. Bucky's hair stood on end like tiny soldiers at attention. I could not see anything. I had no idea why she was in protection mode. Then I noticed almost invisible wavy lines like the ones emanating from a hot pavement on a hundred-degree day. Those wavy lines moved down the hallway right towards us. Bucky continued barking. All her hair stood on end. The hair on the back of my neck began to bristle.

As this thing advanced towards us, swarms of buzzing insects suddenly surrounded me. I am not sure what they were; it was all I could do to scream above them as they circled me. The force of their flight began to blow my hair back. It was so loud that I cried out to God. "Holy Spirit, help me, I need you! Help me! Jesus, save me! I need your help! Father God, come and help me! Please, I cannot fight on my own." I screamed repeatedly from the center of the buzzing storm around me. "Holy Spirit, come Holy Spirit, come Holy Spirit, come!"

And then, God must have flipped a heavenly switch because at once, it all stopped. My hair fell loosely around my shoulders, and the loud buzzing ceased. The wind left me with an audible poof. I sat up in my bed, realizing it had been a dream.

But I knew in my heart it was more than a dream. I felt different. In my dream, the Holy Spirit was helping me as I cried out. I did not understand how to ask God for help, yet in this spiritual battle in my waking hours, the Holy Spirit guided me.

I began to pray before I went to sleep every night after this and asked God for a protected sleep without any kind of influence or attack from the enemy. I prayed that I would be able to speak the name of Jesus under attack and wake up rested and ready for the day to do whatever God had for me.

Over time, I learned to say Jesus' name in my dreams. His name has power. I have not had a nightmare like that in years.

Something beautiful had happened, something extraordinary! Just like in Scripture, where it says that the Lord will fight for us, God had fought for me. From that moment on, I began to dig into the Bible. I wanted to know every promise God had for me. I wanted to know more about who he was. I started getting up at five o'clock in the morning to read Scripture, write notes in my journal, pray, and worship. Whatever God's Spirit did in that nightmare set me on a firm foundation.

As I prayed, I knew for the first time in my life that this enemy of mine existed. I had thought every thought I ever had was my own, but I discovered this was untrue. A lot of times, what I heard was trying to sound like my voice, but it was the enemy speaking.

From then on, I prayed before I went to bed that God would protect me. I learned that when a voice did not align with Scripture, I had to determine where the voice was coming from. And as I began to try to live more like God's Word showed me, I became more able to discern the enemy's voice. When the enemy spoke, he brought thoughts of shame, fear, and confusion, but God's words brought me hope, forgiveness, and peace.

After that, I was not frozen or frightened like in those recurring nightmares I had as a little girl. When anything came against me in a dream, I learned to boldly speak the name of Jesus. That was the key to peaceful rest. His name alone conquered my enemy.

Figuring out the victory I found in Jesus' name also helped me when I was awake. I was learning everything the Bible said was true. This new way of thinking began to change my life.

To say that I was lost before I accepted Jesus is an understatement. It was not just that I didn't know who I was or where I was, but more importantly, I did not know why I was. I didn't understand my purpose. I knew nothing more than mundane day-to-day happenings, most of which I tried to numb.

The burden of childhood trauma is not easily cast off. It lingers in the body, a constant reminder that until it is confronted, felt, and healed, it will not leave. This struggle is one that many of us share, and it is important to acknowledge the weight it carries.

Some people develop sickness because of childhood trauma, and in my case, I ended up diagnosed with three autoimmune diseases: Graves' disease, fibromyalgia, and chronic fatigue syndrome. The stress and emotional turmoil from my past experiences had a profound effect on my physical health. I was also clinically depressed and suffered from severe anxiety.

If you got into my inner circle, I could be funny, innocent, creative, and outgoing, but I had my limits. But if I did not know you, or if I was in a room full of strangers, you would never have known.

After leaving my parents' home, I went to college in New York City. I was both excited and terrified because I had no idea other than a love of writing what I wanted to do with my life. Not knowing God yet showed in every aspect of how I lived.

I had relationships and friendships that were as genuine as I could handle. I had positive experiences and exposure to all kinds of creativity. As life went on, I got further away from ever entering a church on a Sunday morning again. I had gone while living at my parents' house, but I never wanted to go. Church felt sterile and empty. I did not know I could have a relationship with God. It was a struggle to try to please my parents when I was so angry at God. "Why would I want to spend my time singing and talking about a God who didn't even help me when I needed it?" I often said under my breath while the congregation around me sang hymns with a solemnness I could not understand. It was exhausting. It made my heart hurt, and I did not know why. I had been pushing down these feelings for so long I didn't know what healthy felt like. A fierce, hot anger raged inside me, and it was beginning to ball itself together into a mighty fist. Ready to force its way out at any moment. Keeping it in took all the energy I had left. For me, Sunday mornings were for sleeping in.

After God revealed himself to me, I lived differently. God says he is "I AM," referring to himself as being in the present even though he has always been and will always be. He is saying something more in that name. He reminds us that life is at this very moment. Right now, while you are reading these words, you are alive! A few minutes ago was the past, and in a few moments, it will be the future, but right now is the only time you can do something. This understanding of God's presence in the present moment became a guiding principle in my journey of healing and personal growth. Knowing I could stop and talk with him began to turn my fear into faith. "Help me. I am scared, God," I would whisper, now seeing him for who he was, the One who saw me, loved me, and wanted to be with me unconditionally. The lies I had believed about his lack of concern for me had been proven untrue by his love.

Marriage and motherhood did not instantly dispel my inner turmoil as I had hoped. But in the role of a mother, I found a new kind of love that allowed me to embrace my true self for the first time. This transformation, through faith and motherhood, is a testament to the hope that can be found in the most unexpected places.

When I was alone with my first child, I loved her with abandon, innocence, joy, and a deep connection from the very bottom of who I was. I wanted to do everything I could to protect her, provide for her, and keep her innocence intact. I wanted her to get to be a child and experience the fullness of her childhood.

God was working on the hardness of my heart. I did not know yet, but when I look back, this would be the first glimmer of understanding just a little bit of God's love for me.

My first marriage did not last long. It was my choice to divorce; it just felt as if I was taking care of two kids instead of one. It was not my husband's fault; his parents had not raised him in a way that taught him how to step into the role of husband, nor had I understood how to be a wife. It was both of our failures. But I knew how to be a mom, and I wanted my daughter to grow up seeing me happy.

I remember a friend telling me that I was my daughter's example. "If you put up with wrong things," she said, "your daughter will do the same." That advice is why I dared tell my husband I wanted a divorce. I wanted better for my child.

What I did not know then was that no one could fulfill what was missing in me, restore me, or rewrite the story that God had intended for my life. I needed God himself.

I got married a second time, and nine years later, I had a second child, another beautiful example that brought out this part of me that I truly was. I loved being a mom!

I could have done a better job. I was still desperately lost and unhealthy. But a sense of my inner childhood appeared when

I was with my children. All the walls went down like a flower blooming; I felt like me when I was with them. They became my anchors, my reasons to heal.

I have one precious positive memory of God from my childhood. This was before I started fearing the ghosts, which I was told lived in our house.

My flaxen curls were tied back into pigtails with pink ribbons. I remember pulling them softly across my cheek to see the iridescent rainbows they made sparkling in the sunlight. "Wow," I said, my jaw loosely open in awe. "Gosh, you are pretty," I told my ribbons and kissed them sweetly before setting them free to bounce along again with my curls as I skipped across my front yard. The wind was blowing a balmy hug around my tiny frame. I remember stopping to reach my arms around myself and hugging myself tightly.

The air wafted with the sweet perfume of lilacs, and as I breathed them in, I could almost taste them. "Mmmmmm," I said in response to the intoxicating fragrance. Lilacs made me smile. They were so regal, bending down in splendor with the weight of hundreds of tiny blooms. How could something be so beautiful, I wondered. Looking carefully at the blossoms, I could not help but pluck one of the tiny four-petaled heralds of spring. I pressed it firmly against my nose and took the deepest breath I could muster.

I made my way to my favorite place, our cherry blossom tree. That day, it was letting loose its pink splendor to make way for unfurling green leaves. "They look the same as my ribbons," I said proudly to the world around me. A swirl of their beauty wafted around the tree above me like bright pink cotton candy spinning. I remember sticking out my arms as wide as I could, my little hands longing to feel the rush of air against them as I began spinning endlessly.

Like a top set in motion, I just kept turning. If I had to give you a description of the word joy, that was the moment. I felt protected, provided for, at peace, and chock-full of hope. At that moment, I knew exactly who I was. I remember saying, "God, this is perfect. Thank you!" Even though I had only heard about God, part of what I knew about him was that he made me and the things I loved, like my pets, the creek, the flowers, and the birds. That day, I talked to him as if I knew him, and amid all the beauty he had created, his presence was real.

That day, as the petals floated around me, my arms were outstretched, and my tiny dress began filling with air. As I spun, it looked like it was blooming, too. I connected to my Father in heaven through his creation. That is my best memory from that age. What a gift! I am grateful for it.

I continued trying to be a mom and a wife, working hard at doing the things I thought I was supposed to do. I did not connect with the family I grew up in and did not interact with them regularly, but it was easier that way.

I eventually moved closer to my parents' house, about ten minutes away, and at that point, I began to go back to church.

I did not go back to church because I knew Jesus or loved God. I did it for my children. "It should be up to them what they believe," I thought. I started going back to church and had the same old feelings of disengagement, but I tried to connect. I began to serve, and I was not as insular.

"Did anything monumental happen while I was going there?" you might ask. Yes, but it didn't happen in the church. It happened at home. I will tell you all about that in the next chapter, but I would like to end with this: There was never a moment I knew what I was doing other than when I was a mom. Making lunch, tucking kids into bed, reading stories, encouraging little hearts to get back up after they fell, cleaning scraped knees and bandaging them, giving hugs that only a mom can provide, being there as much as I was able to be present, connecting in a way where my kids were allowed to show emotions and feel fully loved just as they were. I tried my best to stand up for them, to protect them, and to help them dream their dreams.

As a mother, I was careful where they were allowed to go. I tried to give them everything I needed from my parents when I was young.

When I was a little girl, I played alone. I grew up on a big property. Across the creek from my house was a Lutheran church and school. Behind the school was a giant field of wild-flowers. On the other side of that field was a road that was about three miles from my home. I remember playing on the school playground, walking through the field, picking flowers, and getting as far as that road. Sometimes my brother came with me. A large farm bell hung on a wooden stand at our house. My mom would ring the bell when it was time to come in for lunch or dinner.

Looking back, I cannot believe I was allowed to wander around alone. I know that's the way it was back then, but I do not understand why I could be alone for so long or what my mom did while I was gone. I cannot imagine letting my children wander like that, but that was my experience. I had this sense of freedom and wonder while out in creation. I know God used that to tell me that I was his. I always loved going down to the creek at the edge of our property, catching salamanders and sitting on the big rock that slanted precariously over the water. I loved looking up at the sky, which made me feel alive. These were precious moments of freedom. They always included creation.

When I divorced my first husband, he eventually got married again. I got married again too. They had more kids, and I had my son.

My second husband had a son from his first marriage, so our family dynamic was chaotic. It got tricky for my daughter because she went back and forth between the two families, and there was so much adjusting for her to do.

I know that we did our best, and I know that I still have not healed completely. I did my best, just like my parents did theirs, as their parents did before them, but I did not know Jesus. I had no idea how to be healthy or whole. I did not know who I was. Life felt fleeting. The days were bland and lacked value some-times. My children were the only thing that gave me some sense of purpose.

I was not doing anything creative at that time. I was not writing, painting, decorating, or repurposing furniture, all of which I love doing now. I muddled through every day, waiting for the moment when I could finally lie down and go to sleep.

During my second marriage, Jesus became my Lord and Savior. Unfortunately, something horrible happened about a week after I was redeemed while battling the enemy over my choice.

When we are born, God deposits everything we need to fulfill our purpose within us, but because we live in a sinful world, life writes over the pages of our hearts with indelible ink, trying its absolute best to reform and reshape us. When we accept Jesus as our Lord and Savior, he washes those pages white. Then, God picks up his pen and begins to write.

Holy plot twists will rewrite our stories using every broken thing, trauma, neglect, regret, and shame. God will use the things meant to defeat us, to reach people who do not know him, and to heal.

Some people will never go to church, and they will not read the Bible. But people will listen to our stories. When our story includes the transforming power of Jesus Christ, we share the hope and love we have found.

Sharing our story is part of our purpose. The great commission commands us to go into the world and make disciples. The Bible gives us examples of these kinds of holy plot twists penned by the hand of God. Everything looks one way, and then God enters, changing it all. Our lives have these moments too. I am telling you about my life to encourage you to share about yours.

Every story is beautiful, valuable, and precious to God. Think about it: The God of creation wants to use every detail in your life to bring him the greatest glory.

God speaks to you in the everyday moments, showing you what he's doing so you can share it with others.

I do not know any Christian who doesn't want to hear the words, "Well done, good and faithful servant." There is nothing we can give Jesus that he doesn't already have except our lives. He will not take them from us; we must offer them to him. There is nothing else we can do to show our gratitude for his grace but dedicate the rest of our existence to finding ways to share about him. His Word is a fire in my bones, and I cannot contain it.

Once we encounter God's perfect love, our hearts want

everyone else to experience it too. How could I not share the gospel? How could I not tell you what God has done for me? Being free is not enough; I want everyone to know this freedom.

Life can be a struggle. I still doubt, but God is always working in me. The truth found in Philippians 1:6 encourages me that God will keep working until the day Christ returns.

Jesus wants to spend time with you. He wants to encourage you, protect you, and provide for you. He has always been with you. In the desperation, in the trauma, in the darkness, he was there. In the depression, in the sadness, he was there. In the numbness, in the running, he was there.

I had opened doors to evil unknowingly giving access to an enemy who hates me. I found myself alone in the darkness far away from anything good. At the bottom of a desolate pit, I cried out and Jesus came to save me.

Chapter Five
Meeting Jesus

• ○ •

Question: If I were to ask you if you had a relationship with Jesus and when you accepted him, do you know when that was?

————o-o-o————

Everything was dark. I was at the bottom of a pit, looking up alone. Completely shut off with no way out, I felt the ache of my loneliness. My forehead dripped with sweat, and my hands shook violently under the heaviness of my realization that I was completely and utterly doomed.

Under the weight of that moment, I surrendered to God. I knew I needed him, and I knew he loved me despite what I had done.

"Where am I, God?" I asked, looking into the utter darkness. "I need you!" I screamed. "Help me! Please help me!" I whispered as the weight of my reality set in. I was nowhere near where I needed to be, and it felt impossible to get out of there. I tried to climb up, but the pit had no walls—just darkness.

Then Jesus appeared at the top of the pit, looking down at me, the bright light from above almost eclipsing his gentle smile. He came down to me swiftly and brought me out, carefully putting my shivering body over his shoulders like the little lost lamb that I was. He pulled me out of the darkness and into the glorious daylight above.

Jesus set my feet on the ground next to his. I could feel the loose dirt between my toes. It was warm from the sun that had been shining on it. Every step brought me comfort. We walked away together, his arm around my shoulders. I was crying inconsolably. Jesus didn't try to tell me anything. Instead, he showed me his love by holding me more tightly as I sobbed. I buried my face in his chest. The soft white robes he wore soothed my skin still hot from my tears. Jesus stroked my hair and patted my back. "Shhhhh, daughter, it is well. I am here. I will never leave you."

I believed him. He would never let me go. I was his. I knew it with every fiber of my being. I was home and safe; a peace I had never known was possible filled my heart.

"This little light of mine, I'm going to let it shine," I sang quietly, feeling the warmth of the holy fire now burning on the altar of my heart. I beamed with love. "This little light of mine, I'm going to let it shine." The words trailed off as my tears stopped falling. I turned and looked into Jesus' eyes. They were gentle pools of compassion overflowing with love and understanding. I felt seen for the first time.

He embraced me and smiled, pulling me close again. "I have been waiting so long for you to come home, my daughter. Welcome home, child, welcome home." And I knew it was true; I was home forever with him.

That was the moment everything changed. I knew what I had believed was wrong. It was all a lie. This was when my unexpected battle began. I had already given my soul to Jesus. I knew it was safe with him, but a war raged around me. It was a battle for my mind.

This choice I made to love Jesus enraged the enemy. I had chosen Jesus. Through this battle, God would show me realities about his power and the enemy's limitations. Overall, I had to endure it.

My daughter Lauren's thirteenth birthday party led to this life-changing moment. It all started with a big slumber party at my mom's house.

Mom's house was the place to have it because I thought ghosts lived there, and they fascinated me. I eventually stopped fearing them as I got older.

My parents exposed me to ghosts, gave me a Ouija board,

told me about aliens, and told me all kinds of things contrary to the Bible. They each grew up with faith, but the world had written over their stories along the way with lies. The Ouija board, a tool for communicating with spirits, was a significant part of my childhood, and its influence continued into my adult life.

We planned the party for Friday the thirteenth and decided to use the Ouija board to make it extra spooky. I cannot believe I served all these young girls on a silver platter to the enemy. I had no idea what I was doing.

The party was fantastic. Everyone was having fun. When we used the Ouija board, we got immediate responses, which was exhilarating. We went into the late hours asking questions.

"What is your name?" we asked in anticipation once we had started speaking with a ghost.

"I am called Eighteen."

"Eighteen? Why?" I asked, fully engaged by this point.

"It is who I am."

"Where are you?" I asked.

"I am in darkness."

We naively tried to make suggestions to help Eighteen out of the dark, thinking we were talking with the spirit of a human, not a demon. We felt sorry for this poor soul trapped in the darkness. Looking back, I can now see that eighteen might have stood for "666," the number used to define the enemy. And where else would he be but in the darkness because there was no light in him? But I was blinded to all this back then.

The feeling of the planchette beneath our fingers was electrifying. It was only a heart-shaped piece of wood, but it pointed with power to the letters that spelled out the answers to the questions in our hearts. "What will the future hold for me?" my daughter asked. We all wanted to know.

Using the Ouija board, we circumvented the One who knows the future. We tried to access unknown knowledge and refused to trust God. Asking God questions hadn't even crossed our minds. I shudder to think about this now.

As we got into our sleeping bags to try to sleep, my daughter's friend Cynthia saw a scary face when she closed her eyes. "Ahhhh!" She sat up, visibly shaken.

"What's wrong?" we asked, leaning forward towards her.

"I saw a man's face. He looks mean. He was scary. He has white skin and a creepy smile. I want to go home," she whispered as tears filled her eyes. We decided to stop. I folded the Ouija board and placed it back in the box with the planchette on top as the girls settled into their sleeping bags on the brightly colored oriental carpet that covered the living room floor.

I gathered the red plastic cups, which were still half full of soda, and the paper plates adorned with pizza crusts and discarded pepperoni slices. Then, I headed to the kitchen. As I walked, I could feel the Ouija board calling to me. How exciting it had been to talk with whomever we were reaching. I imagined an innocent soul caught between the earth and heaven. It was a romanticized moment where I felt awe and wonder. I wanted to know more about what happens after this life is over.

My daughter Lauren and I were both drawn in by what was happening. We thought we were conversing with another part of the universe. I remember feeling bonded with her by the experience.

The worst thing was that we brought the Ouija board home with us. Lauren and I continued using it together. When I say it now, it just seems ridiculous. I can't believe they sell those things in toy stores! To think it was just fun is crazy. But the way I grew up with everybody telling me stories about ghosts, it seemed normal. Lies take root when we are young and impressionable.

These lies forming in our foundation are places where the enemy works to build a place to stay in our lives.

After a while, when I asked questions on the Ouija board, I started getting answers I didn't want. Scary words had replaced the exciting promises for my future. My questions now brought sharp responses. They didn't feel good. They were vindictive. It was as if some sinister character had pushed a button, and suddenly, I was not talking to who I thought I had been talking to anymore. The spirits finally showed me precisely who they were. Like a fish chasing a lure, I was captured, on the hook, and ready to be pulled in.

The last question I asked was from an utterly selfish place. I didn't realize I was being selfish at first. The answer I got was terrifying. I stopped, stood up quickly, flipped the board away, and then threw it in the dumpster outside. I knew that what we had invited in was still in our home.

I wish I had known to pray then. I wish I would have asked Jesus to save me. My daughter and I lived in fear after that day.

The other people in our lives didn't seem to notice what Lauren and I were going through. What I struggled with most were the questions I had asked and my real reasons for asking them. What was wrong with me? Was I a bad person? While pondering these things alone in my living room, I heard a question break through the silence.

"Why do you go to rats?" a voice boomed loudly and as clearly as my own.

"What?" I said aloud, turning nervously to look around the room, rattled by the question and the voice. I don't know how to describe it, but instantly, the truth came into focus in both my mind and my heart. It was like sitting in the optometrist's chair, blind behind blurry lenses, eyes pressed firmly into a static position, until that breathtaking moment when the physician finally clicks the right lens into place, and the words you couldn't read before immediately jump into perfect clarity. Truth unfolded boldly inside me.

I knew I was wrong. Memories rushed in. Everything I had heard about God and his Word flooded my mind like the mighty rushing waters of a tidal wave. They crashed and splashed. Woosh. I was left cleansed and sitting in my right mind.

That is when I met Jesus while I was in the dark pit. I saw it all as if out of my body, watching intently on a giant movie screen in my mind. After he brought me out, we were yoked together. I felt free of the chaos buzzing in the background for as long as I could remember. I was a child of God! The identity I searched for all my life had been right there all the time.

Telling this story reminds me of a Scripture. Colossians 2:11–15 (ESV) says,

In him also you were circumcised with a circumcision made without hands, by putting off the body of the flesh, by the circumcision of Christ, having been buried with him in baptism, in which you were also raised with him through faith in the powerful working of God, who raised him from the dead. And you, who were dead in your trespasses and the uncircumcision of your flesh, God made alive together with him, having forgiven us all our trespasses by canceling the record of debt that stood against us with its legal demands. This he set aside, nailing it to the cross. He disarmed the rulers and authorities and put them to open shame, by triumphing over them in him.

Jesus raised me too! That little girl spinning under the cherry blossom tree had a beautiful eternity ahead of her. She felt safe, at peace, protected, and secure. All I had to do was ask God for help.

I started getting up at five o'clock in the morning, sitting in my kitchen, and praying aloud. I bought my first study Bible, a Thompson Chain Reference Bible. I couldn't get enough of God's Word. I felt hungry and thirsty for more. I learned quickly to ask questions of anyone who knew more about the Bible than I did when I didn't understand something. There was so much to learn!

The Holy Spirit began to speak to me more often, or perhaps I began to hear the Holy Spirit speaking more often. I was still learning which voice was which. I began to understand that the Holy Spirit always brought life when he spoke. Sometimes, I felt a conviction about how I was living. It came in a way that brought me back to God. His kindness and truth shone through the darkness of my old ways.

I remember being sick not long after all of this happened. The virus had settled deep into my lungs. As I sat inhaling the medicine from my nebulizer treatment, I heard,

Remember all the years you willingly inhaled the death of cigarette smoke? You anxiously drew its toxins deeply into your lungs. Was it a bad habit? Addiction? Rebellion? Unbelief? Anxiety? Discontentment? Yes, all of these and more, my child. It hurt my heart to see you choose death. You ran to it with hearty anticipation. You convinced yourself it calmed you; it helped you; you couldn't live without it. You assured yourself it wasn't harming you. Remember the day you heard me ask you to stop?

I closed my eyes as I inhaled the medicine. The loud rushing gurgle of the nebulizer machine drowned out the TV show I had been watching. Instantly, I was transported back to that day. "Yes," I said with remorse in my heart. I remember driving while my son was in his car seat. The window was down to keep the smoke outside of the car. I held the cigarette between my fingers and watched as the rushing air intensified its fiery tip. It looked like the embers of a campfire. Smoke blew back so quickly I couldn't see it until I brought my arm back inside the car window to take a drag. I inhaled with my lips tightly around the filter until my cheeks sunk in deeply on either side.

Catching a glimpse of myself in the sideview mirror, I exhaled. "Throw it out the window," I heard. Before I knew it, I was chucking the cigarette out of the window. I watched the smoke curl, and it dissipated before my eyes. I reached down and put up the window, focusing on the road before me. "That was your last one," I heard clearly and silently agreed.

I had tried quitting so many times, but there was an urgency about quitting that came with this voice. I never smoked again. Not only was I able to stop, but the smell of cigarettes made me feel sick to my stomach after that day. It felt like a miracle, and I was free.

The heart makes idols out of anything and everything. I heard the voice of truth through the chaos and the crazy parade of deadly lies that marched loudly through my mind for most of my life. As the days went on, I regained the flavor I hadn't even noticed had become dulled. I could run again, dance again, and smell beautiful fragrances again. A new world I had blotted out sprung back to life around me. It bothered me that I had been so readily willing to settle for death.

As the memory faded, I looked back at the TV in front of me. Picking up the remote control, I switched the power off. "Breathe in deeply. Breathe deeply that which brings life. Choose me. Run after me. Be convinced that you can't live without me. Be much with me!"

I heard God lovingly invite me even closer to him. I will never use my nebulizer without remembering this. "Thank you, Lord, for speaking the truth with a tangible reminder. I choose you!" I said and meant it.

I haven't told you the most incredible part of this redemption story. On the same day, in the same house, in a different room, my daughter met Jesus too. Every year, we celebrate together. Talk about a holy plot twist! Look at what God has done. He took the temptation the enemy gave us and used it instead for our good. We asked the enemy, but ultimately, it was God who answered.

Just when the evil one thought he had my daughter and me all wrapped up and twisted, with our lives set in a direction that would never include Jesus, the Holy Spirit found us in our most vulnerable moments and convicted us of our sins. We admitted our need for Jesus. We asked him to be our Savior. We knew we needed him. And he came to us.

In one snap of God's fingers, we went from hell on earth to being safely held by Christ forever.

God uses what was meant for evil for good. He will use whatever it takes to get his children home with him.

How amazing it was for God to restore us at the same time. When Lauren and I finally told each other what happened, it was the most bonding experience I've had with any other human being. We were reborn at the same time. My daughter, whom I gave birth to, was now my sister in Christ. God writes miraculous stories!

My depression and anxiety were gone. Instead, there was joy. I felt outgoing and became tenacious. All I wanted to talk about was Jesus. The thing that had been missing from my life was his unconditional love, his closeness, and his peace; it was his presence. It was him!

I am still growing. How amazing is that? I am still growing and becoming more like Jesus every day. I still wake up with the thirst and hunger I had initially. God is teaching me how to be healthy. He has taken my sick places and healed them.

God has rewritten my story and revived my soul, and I want to tell everyone about him. I wanted to show those who don't feel purpose in their lives that God will use even the difficult things to draft their stories. He will change the things that look broken and lost into something good. He takes what has shattered and puts it back together, creating something new.

God throws a broken cup back on the potter's wheel, stretching and smoothing it to form something that will pour his love into many cups. There is a Japanese art called kintsugi, in which artists take a broken vessel and repair it with gold. Not only is the new creation more beautiful, but it is more valuable, and the places that had been the weakest become the strongest. God, our Creator, reworks us, making new creations from the pieces of life that the world has shattered. Only God could make what seems useless to us invaluable. Only God can bring new purpose and beauty from ashes.

God will continue working as he promised in Philippians 1:6. Until then, Jesus sits at the Father's right hand, interceding on our behalf. I will never fully understand it. I guess if I could, he wouldn't be God.

Some think the only way to accept Jesus is to be in a church. But you can do it anywhere. Wherever you are, when your heart is open and ready to accept the truth, Jesus is poised to walk into your heart forever.

God continues to write Jesus' story in all his children's hearts. Nothing is too complicated for God to transform. That is his specialty.

As a podcast host, I can attest to the power of our stories and the unmistakable hand of God at work in our lives. We all need to share our stories. I don't have enough weeks in my life, even if I podcast until the day I die, to share everyone's story, but if I can connect with you through this book, who knows how many people I can reach?

My desire is for you to learn how to share your story. I want you to feel confident and bold. I want you to see the things you may have missed and to know the goodness of who God is.

Have you ever wondered why we have a story to tell? Did you ever consider how God wants us to use our stories? Have you found the courage to let him be in charge? God won't force us to come to him; he always allows us to choose.

For many years, I tried to write my own story. God's story is much better! God has done more than I could think or imagine.

In the Bible, God gives unending examples of times when he asks his people to do things that don't make sense. God's way provides him with glory when the story is over.

Would you expect God to open a sea you could walk through? Or could you predict that once you got to the other side, God would use the same water that set you free to kill the enemies who followed you?

Would you imagine that God would come to the earth he created and be born as a tiny, helpless infant consenting to spend years growing up confined by humanity and then spend three years trying to explain who he was to people who didn't understand?

Could you imagine a God willing to die on the cross to atone for our sins? His love is strong enough to bring us back into a relationship with himself. More than that, he was willing to take our punishment even though he was holy.

God's love, 1 Corinthians 13 love, differs from ours. There is no agenda. It looks at the heart of others first and puts aside its desires and needs. It ministers to the wounded. This is the love God loves us with. This is the love that Jesus took to the cross.

Jesus says that when we walk with him, his yoke is easy, and his burden is light. He uses our story to carry his story to those who don't know him, wanting everyone to know the truth. This is why the world needs to hear your story.

The Bible says we are the aroma of Christ, the fragrance of life to some, and death to others. We carry around the aroma of his presence.

The invitation to become Christ's fragrance and emit him to the world around us is incredible! Your story could bring life to people who would otherwise spend eternity separated from a loving God.

In Jesus' day, they would anoint a king's royal robes with perfume. One of the quickest ways people recognized a king wasn't by his crown or his scepter, but by his royal aroma. God wants to anoint you with a scent that brings life wherever you go.

What I didn't know as a new Christian was that God was going to ask me to minister to unexpected people. God started with my ex-husband and his wife. He asked me to share his love with them and their children. In the next chapter, see how doing things God's way changed everything.

Chapter Six
God Changed My Heart

———————— • O • ————————

Question: Have you ever felt like God was talking to you? Have you ever noticed or heard things in your heart that felt like they came from God, and if so, what were they?

————o-o-o————

"Tell her now," I heard God say deep in my heart. It was so loud that I turned around, thinking someone had entered the bedroom. But as I sat quietly journaling, more words came spilling like fresh water onto the pages. "Tell her I want all of her heart," God continued. "I want all of her! I want her heart, her attention, and her trust. I am faithful. I am her good Father!"

As I scanned the words I had written, my heart began to break for my first husband's wife. "God, I don't know how to tell her this," I said as I closed my eyes and opened my hands before my chest. My palms were facing upward, and I imagined them ready to receive whatever God had for me. "Lord, it's hard enough," I said, crying. "Why do you want so much from me?"

As soon as I said it, I regretted it. I knew, in theory, that if God asked me to do something, it would be the best thing for me, but the part of me that learned to be a people pleaser as a young girl struggled with his request. It was bad enough that my past included two ex-husbands.

But God had helped me connect with this family by learning to pray for them and to try to be a loving part of their lives. I didn't want to lose that, not just for me, but for my daughter Lauren. Being close to her dad and stepmom meant more peace and comfort for her. It wasn't her fault that I divorced her father.

I reached over to my phone and put on worship music. The soothing melodies and uplifting lyrics helped me connect with God and find the courage to obey his direction. I listened to the music and sang along, intermittently whispering, "I can if you help me, God. I can if you help me." Encouragement and love filled my heart. Rays of warm sunlight shone through the window and onto my face. It felt as if God had stepped into the room. The way my words mingled with the music playing filled me with faith to give God my worry and trust him with it.

"Here," I said, eyes still closed, standing barefoot at the edge of my bed. "I give it all to you, God, because I trust you." I extended my arms, raising them towards the ceiling. "You know what is best for me. I trust you," I said one more time as I let go of fear about what could happen when I shared God's words with her.

"I am going to do it now," I said out loud to help convince myself that I was going to call her. I had learned the importance of obeying God's direction. *Ring, ring, ring.* The sound of the phone pulsed rhythmically in my ear. *Where is she?*

I knew in my spirit the words God wanted me to say, and I felt an urgency to say them. I knew it would be weird; so many things could go wrong, but the urgency felt like a fire trapped in my stomach. It was so intense that all I wanted was relief.

God had it all planned. I was in church that Sunday, and she came and sat right next to me. "Hi," I said sweetly, leaning in to hug her. "Where is everyone else?"

"Everyone is sick, but I am fine so far, and I felt like I needed to be here," she responded. "It's so weird. I can't wait to see what the sermon is about. I can't shake the feeling that God has something important to say to me today."

"Boy, does he," I murmured under my breath. The queasy, fiery feeling began to burn again right in the pit of my stomach. "Here, God?" I asked quietly as we began to sing the first worship song. I resisted leaning over to say the words God had asked me to share as long as possible. Focused on God, I raised my hands towards heaven, and my spirit praised the Lord.

"Say it now," God said. I jumped back, opened my eyes, startled, and looked around the sanctuary. Alarmed and on edge, I closed my eyes again.

"Do it now. Say it now. Tell her, tell her, tell her," God said. The fire in my stomach erupted like lava from a volcano. I couldn't take the pressure. I leaned over and touched her shoulder and whispered God's words into her ear. "Whew," I sighed, followed by immediate relief from the urgency. I closed my eyes and praised God again, not knowing the implications of what I had just done.

After my marriage failed, my daughter and I had moved into our own apartment, and I began over again without my husband. I promised myself I would work diligently to preserve my daughter's relationship with her father. It was the hardest thing I ever did. Over the years, it has gotten more manageable.

We lived several blocks from each other, which made it easy for Lauren to see both families. New siblings were born, and things got more complicated, but we persevered. We shared Lauren's care, responsibilities, and bills for braces, extra-curricular activities, and new school clothing. We all got along most of the time, but when we did not, it was stressful. Lauren's dad and I had many disagreements, and over time, his new wife and I would end up on the phone trying to smooth things out.

His new wife became part of my family; I went out of my way to tell her that I appreciated Lauren having another woman who loved her. I sent notes, and we had phone conversations in which I intentionally tried to express my gratitude. It was the most important thing I could do for all of us.

Sometimes, it was difficult. This woman was ten years younger than I was. Her long dark hair was straight and smooth. I always secretly wanted to have straight hair. My wild blonde curls were hard to control. No matter what I did, I never got the same hairstyle twice. Friends, even some family members, said I shouldn't like her. The world told me she was somehow my competition and my enemy, but the world was wrong.

We would have been friends in another set of circumstances. We both loved to knit and crochet. We each liked plants and decorating and had a unique sense of style. I desperately wanted to like the other woman helping raise my daughter. I hadn't accepted Jesus yet, but this concept of loving others had always been part of my personality.

As the years passed, I realized I genuinely loved everyone in my ex-husband's family. This love was deep and moved me to tears when I prayed for them. One of the first things God told me to do was to pray for their family. "Lord, please bless Lauren's dad and stepmom. I know you have a good plan for them. Our family needs you to bring unity. Would you do something special to bless them today, so they know who you are?" I prayed honestly, wanting a storehouse of blessings for them. The love I felt in my heart surprised me as much as it energized me. "Wow, God, you are making me new, just like you promised," I got up from where I had been kneeling. "I only want to love you and love the people around me. Lord, I want to reach a multitude for your kingdom," I whispered with a powerful sense of purpose. "I want everyone to know you, Lord. Thank you. Thank you for loving me!"

It was a freeing, peaceful feeling that bubbled up deep within my newly formed heart in Christ. It was awesome! But no one, and I mean no one, I talked about these new feelings with understood.

I was supposed to hate my ex-husband, his new wife, and their children. But I fought like a salmon swimming upstream against the violent currents of the culture around me. Repeatedly, I dismissed thoughts of insecurity, envy, or comparison. I went out of my way to be loving. I offered help whenever I could if their family was in need.

Some years later, my family moved from the church I grew up in to a new church. From the very first service, I knew I was home. This church read the Bible verse by verse, had a discipleship program, and were active in missional living. They had numerous small groups, a fantastic youth group, and a healthy college-aged ministry.

One day, I was talking with Lauren's stepmom, and she sounded hungry like I had been. Even though she attended a church and was incredibly involved, I could tell something was missing. I invited her to come to my church's prayer and praise night. She came that Wednesday night, and everything began to change. She loved it, and her kids loved the activities provided for them. My ex-husband worked on Wednesday nights and was not able to attend. After a while, I suggested that the family might be able to handle one Sunday morning a month too. There were four kids at their house, and they lived forty-five minutes from the church, so I knew that it would be a challenge. But I also knew they were supposed to be there.

They began coming, and soon they came every Sunday. Lauren, for the first time in her life, had a place where her entire family came together once a week. It was wonderful. I paid careful attention to avoid making anything awkward for my ex-husband, and over time, everyone settled into the new church family.

Little did I know that God had just started healing our families. My ex-husband's wife and I spent hours on the phone as her faith came to life. She had gone to church her whole life but never gave everything to Jesus. That was when God gave me the words to share with her about wanting all her heart.

On her ride home that day, she processed what I had whispered to her during worship time at church. Then I got the phone call I was so worried about. "Hello," I said, my voice cracking.

"Hi Amanda," she said abruptly. "Listen, I just have to know," she said, stammering. "Why, why did you say that? Why would you say that to me?" She was crying.

"Oh, please don't cry! I never wanted to make you cry. I love you." I started to cry too.

"Well, I don't want you to cry either," she said, sniffling.

I reached for a tissue from the box on the table next to my couch. The tissue felt soft and comforting against my skin.

As I began to blow my nose, the sound that came out surprised me and shattered the awkward silence. *THHHHH-HHHH.* It sounded like a giant somewhere had let loose horrible gas. I was thoroughly embarrassed by the noise. The sound of uncontrollable laughter came rumbling over the phone line. I burst out laughing too.

"Are you okay?" I asked lovingly.

"Yes, she answered peacefully.

"The words were not mine. They were from God," I said. "I know it's hard to believe, but—"

"I do believe you! That is what I needed to hear." We talked for hours after that, sharing our hearts and our struggles.

I asked her if I could disciple her, and she said yes. Since then, we have entered that deep and sacred relationship, and many amazing things have happened. She got baptized, as did my ex-husband and their children.

We have come to love each other as sisters. We are family. People who have seen us talking, laughing, and hugging each other with no idea who we are to each other always responded in awe. God has restored our family. Amazing. God's love is stronger than broken families!

We even went on a mission trip to Africa with my daughter. My church filmed a short video about this part of my testimony. Hurting people approached me for months afterward about learning to love the "difficult" people in their lives.

Of all the people I have ever mentored, this relationship was closer and more profound than any other. God's command to pray for their family produced an abundant, fruitful harvest that continues to grow.

I got divorced again. Since my second husband and I were never able to reconcile, I will forever be grateful to God for redeeming my relationship with my first husband and his family. My second husband dealt with mental health and addiction issues, which kept our family from healing, but I believe God continues to pursue him, too. We pray for him and want whatever restoration God might have if he ever can get into recovery and have a healthy relationship with us.

My greatest desire is to be good soil. Mark 4:20 (NLT) says, "And the seed that fell on good soil represents those who hear and accept God's word and produce a harvest of thirty, sixty, or even a hundred times as much as has been planted."

I want to have a life that produces a harvest for God's kingdom. I am thankful for this profound opportunity he gave me as part of my testimony. I love sharing this story of healing, redemption, and love. God promises living the ways he tells us will produce eternal fruit. And it has!

Sometimes the process of growing that harvest means pulling up deep roots, pruning bare branches, and weeding the garden of our hearts. I never would have predicted how God would accomplish these things in me.

In the next chapter, I share the story of my fiftieth birthday. There was no party. I received no lavish presents. No one even made me breakfast in bed. I would describe it as one of the worst days of my life. Until, that is, God showed me the day from a totally different perspective. The sharp and painful parts were his careful pruning. In the end this day was a priceless gift. It was a day of miraculous freedom!

Chapter Seven
My Fiftieth Birthday Present

—————————————— • ○ • ——————————————

Question: Have you had any significant losses, such as the death of grandparents, friends, or other people who were important to you? Maybe the loss was a relationship, a dream, or your innocence. Do you remember what you felt at that time?

—————o-o-o—————

Grrrrrrrrrr. A deep, sinister growl echoed in the misty morning air. I turned quickly to see what was heading our way. And as I did, Eva, my sweet little Chihuahua, pulled her leash out of my hand and sprinted off like a wild animal. "No, Eva, come back here," I yelled at the top of my lungs. It was six o'clock in the morning, and my neighbors' lights started to go on like popcorn, popping one after another until every light beamed in the dark sky.

Eva ran faster than I'd ever seen a dog run. I kept screaming, "Eva, Eva, come to Mommy." Bleary-eyed, with no makeup on, I stood disheveled in my mismatched pajamas and bent low to the ground. Spreading my arms wide open, I called her again. "Eva, I love you! Please *stop!*"

She didn't even look back at me. Brokenhearted and defeated, I fell forward with my forehead resting in the palms of my hands. "Why God? Why would you let this happen, too? Isn't this day bad enough?" I pleaded, beginning to well up with tears. "My phone," I blurted out, breaking my desperation. Realizing I had it in my pocket, I called my son, Jackson, who was inside. "Jackson, Eva ran away; get out here and help me!" I struggled to stand up again.

Jackson came barreling through the front door like a super-hero. "Mom, which way did she go?"

"That way." I pointed as Eva headed for the road. Both of us shuddered, realizing how close she was to it. "Eva, no! Stop!" We yelled in unison, sounding like a stereo on full blast. I ran after Eva, calling her name at the top of my lungs. "Call Lauren!" I yelled, and Jackson quickly hit speed dial to call my daughter, who was supposed to come to our house to take him to school later. Suddenly, Eva turned away from the road and headed back toward us.

"She's coming back." I squealed with joy. "Yes, yes, she's going to come back!" I bent down, ready to scoop her up, as she ran towards my arms. But in her anxious stupor, she flew past me.

"No!" I cried. Jackson and I ran around the neighborhood, catching glimpses of her between houses. Our neighbors stood harried and wrinkled at their front doors, wondering why we had been yelling. After we told them about Eva, everybody was looking for our precious eight-pound dog.

I looked at my watch, and my stomach sank when I realized I had to go back inside. This was the morning of my fiftieth birthday, the day I had to drive an hour to Pottstown to take my husband to rehab one last time. Devastated, I turned the search for Eva over to my son just as Lauren appeared in the driveway.

"What's going on?" she asked, and Jackson filled her in while I headed to the front door.

My husband and I had to be two of the first people at the facility for him to be seen, and if I didn't leave on time, he would have nowhere to stay. As I slowly climbed the stairs into my home, my muscles felt rubbery and weak from all the running. My throat was dry, and my heart felt dry too. "Happy birthday to me," I said softly as I headed to my bedroom to get dressed.

I put my clothes on and grabbed my knitting bag to have something to do while waiting at the facility. "Come on, we have to leave now," I said to my husband, and we got into the car. I can't even describe the sour, twisting pit in my stomach. My baby, my sweet, tiny dog was out there, alone and scared. All I could think of was that we lived right next to a creek and a road.

I clamped my hand firmly on the key and slid it into the ignition. Turning it forward and hearing the engine roar on, I realized I was holding my breath. I let it out slowly through my pursed lips and turned towards my husband. "I don't want to talk at all," I said abruptly and began to pray aloud. He still tried to talk to me several times. I rudely put my hand out, my arm outstretched, fingers facing the sky, and shouted, "Quiet." I prayed, thanking God in advance for bringing my puppy home. When I prayed this way, it showed my faith that God could do anything. I trusted him to do so.

We drove the rest of the time in silence. When we arrived, there was no one in the parking lot. I shifted the car into park, and when I let go, my hand shook. I turned to my husband. "Please get out and go up to the door to wait. I will be there in a minute," I said sternly. He got out of the car. I prayed again, "God, I know you can do anything. Thank you in advance for bringing Eva home." I opened my car door slowly, wanting to be anywhere else but at another rehab. I joined my husband at the front door, and we waited awkwardly for them to open it.

It felt like hours, but it was only minutes before I got a text from my kids. Carefully, I pulled my phone out of my back pocket to see who was texting me. I turned away from the door and started walking across the parking lot. There was a picture of Jackson and Lauren. Jackson was holding Eva! They were all huddled together in front of the police station. "Yes God, yes! You did it!" I shouted joyfully, stomping hard onto the stone ground beneath my feet. "Whew," I sighed deeply, not realizing how afraid I had been that God wouldn't come through for me. Somehow, those feelings about the puppy were mixed with my thoughts about God not healing my husband, and the lack of faith saddened me. I prayed in advance, thanking God, but deep within my heart, a little girl still felt wary to trust him with her pain and fear.

Ring. I wrestled in my pocket for my ringing phone. "Hello?" I answered quickly,

"Mom, we got her. Did you see the text?" My daughter asked.

"Yes, oh yes, thank you for getting her!" I forgot for just a moment where I was and why I was there.

"She ran two miles away," my daughter continued. "A man found her, brought her into his house, gave her water, and then took her to the police station."

"Thank you for calling the police, Lauren," I said, not knowing that I would have been so level-headed to do so myself. "I will call you later. Just let Jackson stay home from school. I'll call him out now. Thank you two. I love you both so much." I returned to the front door.

While I was on the phone, a rehab employee pulled in and unlocked the door. She was already talking to my husband. This was how I celebrated my fiftieth birthday: walking numbly behind my husband into the building, where they would hopefully find him a place with a bed.

The day before everything had fallen apart. My husband showed signs of struggling with bipolar disorder for years. He self-medicated with alcohol and became an alcoholic.

God and I argued a lot over whether my husband should stay or go, and honestly, I was angry at God. What did he want from me anyway?

Looking back, I can see now what God was doing during those years. God used this struggle to forge my faith. He was my refuge and my provider. He stepped in as my heavenly husband.

Even though I could see the good things God was doing, it didn't take away the horrible pain, the feeling of always waiting for another shoe to drop, the feeling as if I was walking on eggshells. All I wanted to do was sleep and forget about it.

During those years, my autoimmune diseases began. I'm sure I was clinically depressed. I don't like to think back to that time. It felt like being stabbed in the back by the person who was supposed to protect me.

And when I accepted Jesus, instead of being happy for me, my husband seemed to hate Jesus. He didn't want me to be who I had become. He wanted the old, broken version of me he had married.

I guess I can understand from his perspective; we were a dysfunctional couple. And once I wanted to get healthy, it scared him. I am so grateful for Jesus and having somewhere to go in the chaos.

I couldn't go to my kids—they were kids. I couldn't go to my parents. I tried, but they didn't understand. I couldn't go to my friends; they didn't seem to get it either. No one knew what to say or what to do, so I kept my struggles in, and I started to become numb.

Our home was loud and chaotic because of living with an alcoholic. I was trying to live more like Jesus. During that time, it felt as if the enemy would use my husband to chastise me. It was as if all the rage of the enemy was coming out of my husband's mouth some days.

The day before my birthday, my husband called to tell me that the car wasn't working and he was stranded in the parking lot at work, so I went to pick him up. We left the car, and as we were driving home, I could smell the liquor and cigarettes on his breath. "Were you drinking at work?"

"No," he said, slurring his words. His eyes had that familiar glassy glaze, and I could see he was inebriated. He never admitted he was drunk. The dishonesty felt almost as bad as the drinking.

"I can't do this anymore," I screamed as I drove faster. "How could you do this again?" I started to cry.

The amount of money he made at that job was nothing compared to when we first got married. Before he started drinking, he was a talented art director with a distinguished career. Pulling into our driveway, I felt disgusted, defeated, and determined to get him out of our home. "Go to the bedroom and wait for me; I need to check on the kids," I said. I was exhausted.

I walked into the bedroom, and he was undressing. I watched as he tried to balance and fell back onto the bed. He had bruises all over his body. How did it get this bad, I wondered, knowing those bruises were the signs of his liver shutting down.

"I know you're drinking, and you have to leave. I will see if any beds are available at a rehab anywhere. If you're willing to go,

I will take you."

After searching everywhere I knew from all the other times he went to rehab, I found a place in Pottstown, an hour away from our house. They didn't have a bed, but they had walk-in spots—just a few, available only first thing in the morning. That place was all I could find available, so I took it. He agreed to let me check the bedroom to make sure there was no more alcohol hidden anywhere, and I let him go to sleep. I slept in the living room. I hadn't slept in the bedroom in years.

I got up early in the morning. I roused our little Chihuahua and went for a walk. As I told you, I started my day off with her running away.

After entering the rehab center, I was ushered to the waiting room. This wasn't my first time; I knew it would be an all-day event, so I brought my knitting and a book. I was knitting a new felted bag. It was full of beautiful, bright colors with a golden background. I intentionally made it large because I would be felting it, a process that shrinks the knitting. Felting is amazing. I would eventually take the bag, put it in hot, soapy water in the washing machine, and agitate it. The process shrinks down the wool, thickens it up, and makes it usable. I remember praying as I knit. It reminded me of when I made prayer shawls, with my hopes and dreams woven into every stitch.

I sat knitting for hours. Finally, someone came out and talked to me. They had found a place with a bed, but there was no way to get my husband there. Sometimes, an ambulance picks patients up, but in this case, I had to drive him. I wasn't sure I could handle another forty-five minutes. We started at six o'clock in the morning, and I wouldn't be done until after five o'clock at night.

I got the address from the receptionist. We didn't have GPS on our phones yet, so it was nerve-wracking trying to find the place, but I finally did. There was total silence in the car, besides me praying or listening to worship music. I refused to have any interaction. I just needed to get him somewhere safe so that I could be free. I knew that this was the last time.

We finally got to the facility. I handed my husband the duffle bag I had packed the night before. I made an appointment at the front desk afterward to have whoever ended up being his therapist contact me because the children and I had decided that we were going to tell my husband he was not welcome in our home anymore. I wanted his set of keys back.

I made my way home. The sun was going down. It was an exhausting day. The only good things that happened on my fiftieth birthday so far were that I had finished the bag I was knitting and that Eva had returned home safely. I thought, "This is my declaration, my tangible marker of this season ending. I give it to you, God."

When I got home, my kids hugged me, and I felt significantly better. The atmosphere in my home felt like freedom. The heaviness had lifted from my shoulders; I felt light. I went into the living room.

When my husband used to scream and yell obscenities in a drunken rage, I would sit in this same room. It was the furthest room away from his. I remember covering my ears and praying loudly, "God, I need peace. Please bring me peace. Whatever I must do for your peace, Lord God. Do not let those horrible things stick. Please make my heart like Teflon so that everything spoken over me will slide off instead of sticking."

God had finally answered my prayers. As much as he made my heart slippery, many things screamed at me had stuck. I had a lot of healing to do; I needed to find out who I was again.

That night with my children, the people who had made me most like myself, finally felt like my birthday. This was my present from God.

I collapsed on the couch, just beginning to relax, and my daughter handed me a beautiful little book. "I got your friends to write you letters about how they feel about you for your birthday," she said, smiling radiantly. "I started months ago."

Lauren opened the book for me to see it. I sat up and motioned for the kids to snuggle beside me on the couch.

"I just printed them out and put them together so you could know how much we all love you."

What had I done to deserve kids like mine? "Oh, Lauren, thank you!" I reached over to hug her.

Outside of the home, I was vibrant, joyful, and alive, and that's the person everyone talked about in these letters. I looked at the first one; it read,

How can I best describe what my friend, Amanda, means to me on her fiftieth birthday? If I had the space available, I could share at least fifty ways, one for each year, that Amanda blesses me and the people who know and love her. Instead, I will share a few of her most amazing characteristics. First, Amanda is kind. She genuinely cares about people and how we are doing. Next, Amanda is joyful. When you're around her, her joy is contagious. You can't help but feel better when you're with her. Finally, Amanda loves the people in her life unconditionally and sacrificially. She always puts their needs before her own. She brings out the best in others because she loves them well, believes in them, and goes the extra mile to support them in any way she can. I'm grateful and honored to call Amanda my friend and sister in the Lord. Love you, my dear friend. Happy birthday!

Oh, my goodness, I thought. How beautiful! And I turned the page to read the following letter:

Happy fiftieth, Amanda! I remember back when we first met, and I already had an impression that you were a godly woman who was filled with passion for Jesus and his kingdom. Getting to know you revealed so much more about how you choose to live your life according to the Bible and how you seek God first in the good and bad of everyday life. You taught me to recognize when God is speaking, even in the little things. Having done spiritual warfare together for our church and families bonded us in a way that even later being separated by multiple states couldn't break. I'm so thankful you were everything you seemed to be and so much more! Our friendship has blessed me greatly, and I'm excited to see what God continues doing through you. Keep shining for him. Love you, sweet friend!

Wow, God used this book, my daughter's heart, and my friends' words in his perfect timing. His holy plot twist turned what could have been the worst day in my life into an affirmation of the good he was doing in me.

Message after message had me blubbering with disbelief at how others saw me. They saw me as bold, talented, empathetic, compassionate, loving, and kind—things I didn't feel I had been for so long. Warm tears welled up slowly and fell, dripping quietly on my cheeks. "Thank you," I said, knowing I would cherish this moment always.

After I finished reading the book, my kids and I entered the bedroom together. This had been my husband's room. We hauled his things outside and threw them in a dumpster. We prayed over the room and anointed it with oil. I stayed up until three o'clock in the morning, painting the walls and making a safe space to claim for myself.

I got the keys back from my husband. We sent him off to try to find himself and a healthy life. He never stepped foot back into our home again. We ended up getting divorced. I now had two ex-husbands. Unfortunately, God has not redeemed this marriage.

We tried as a family to love him from afar, and we would visit him. It always led to feelings of sadness, and he never kept the boundaries we asked for. I had to ask him to write letters because it was upsetting to all of us when we spoke on the phone. He could not do that consistently either. Over time, my children and I gave up.

We never stopped praying for him. I still hope he finds Jesus, but his narcissistic, emotionally toxic behavior never changed. Choosing to be healthy, we closed the door to the relationship.

Eventually, his son from his first marriage, who we stayed in touch with, also suffered from bipolar disorder and addiction. Sadly, he died by suicide three years ago.

We all took part in the funeral. Jeffrey's mom had us ride with her. My daughter and I shared Scriptures from the pulpit at the service. My son carried his casket. My ex-husband knew about the funeral, but he didn't come.

Have you experienced an event like my fiftieth birthday? Can you look back on that time and glean the treasure from the ashes? Often, God takes the mundane and makes it miraculous, just as he did for me.

Are you ready? God has a plan to take what looks dead and bring life to it. God confounds the enemy through our transformations and reaches the world for his kingdom. Will you partner with God and step into his plan for your life?

In my life I have found God often moves in ways that look like the wrong direction. We simply cannot understand his perspective. We must learn to trust his character more than our circumstances. In the next chapter I will tell you about the time God showed me this truth in a radical way. As unexpected as the situation was, he used it to be certain it would be a lesson I would never forget.

Chapter Eight

What Looked Like the

Wrong Direction

—————————— • ○ • ——————————

Question: Do you ever notice things that seem out of place?

————o-o-o————

"Oh, my goodness," I said aloud. "What is he doing? He is going to get hit!"

I watched intently, as we all tend to watch potential accidents, with my eyes glued to the giant steel snowplow recklessly careening down the road. It was menacing in size compared to the tiny, colorful cars around it, making them look like play toys. The sun shone through the storm clouds, a bright shaft from heaven gleaming onto the metal plow. It was like something out of a movie. I sat in my car watching it all unfold, not a part of any of the action but feeling as if I were.

As I waited in the drive-through bank line, snow was lilting down softly around me and accumulating on my car. It was quiet and peaceful in that moment. Feeling frozen in time, I leaned my head back for a moment and closed my eyes. In my mind, I could see a scene from winter long ago. My husband had gone outside to walk the dog and, while out there, had stomped through the snow drifts to spell out my name. He called me proudly to look out the living room window. And when I looked through the frost-covered pane, there it was, A M A N A D A. I chuckled, opening my eyes. Remembering that he had gotten lost in spelling my name, I said, "AH - Man - A - Duh instead of Amanda," cracking myself up. My family has called me that playfully ever since. "Why did he have to start drinking and ruin it all," I thought. A knot tightened in my stomach.

I looked back out the window. The plowed piles of snow in the parking lot around me had been covered with a soft, fresh powder, making the entire lot look like God had carefully spread out an ivory down comforter to lie on. As I put my window down, the icy air entered, battling the toasty warm air from the heater. "Brrrr." I shook my shoulders back and forth. My leather gloves squeaked as I gripped the steering wheel tightly. "This weather is stupid," I said, as if someone else were in the car to hear me and agree. "What's taking so long?" I pushed the button to close the window again. As the window went up, a new worship song began to play on the radio, filling the car with a different kind of warmth. That's when I saw it.

A snowplow was backing up in full-on traffic. I watched in disbelief as cars swerved to get around him. He was moving slowly and steadily backward along the right-hand side of the road. The driver raised his massive metal plow, and I could hear a faint backup signal beeping into the cool air. *Beep, beep, beep.* I watched, my eyes glued to the truck. Leaning forward and gripping my steering wheel tightly, I heard myself gasping. "No, stop!"

Somehow, he maneuvered backward without hitting any cars. He was so big and heavy that he would have totaled anything he hit. When the truck finally came to rest, he was almost out of my view. That is when his plow came down. I watched in panic as he lowered it to the ground. Thud! It shook the parking lot when it landed on the icy road. Reverberations rippled out in every direction. It was as if a Tyrannosaurus rex trampled through our world. The giant thud shook me to the core.

Cars whizzed by him as he sat still and silent. He began to plow the snow that had drifted onto the side of the road. It had not been visible from my vantage point, but he had seen it. He pushed and plowed and cleared the way. I watched other drivers notice what he was doing, and they began to follow him in the clear lane.

I hadn't noticed that all the cars had become bottlenecked into one lane before he plowed. Things would have gotten even more dangerous if he hadn't come along and dislodged the obstruction. It would have been worse to leave the road obstructed than to have driven backward as he did.

Sitting there contemplating what I had just seen, I realized that sometimes God goes backward amid oncoming traffic for us. It feels dangerous. It seems wrong, but what if going backward is the best way?

Sometimes, we think, "Oh my goodness, what is he doing?" when God begins to back up to help us dislodge something that has drifted onto our path. An obstruction can keep us from moving forward if he doesn't clear it.

As I sat there in awe, God reminded me of the words from Luke 9:62 (ESV): "No one who puts his hand to the plow and looks back is fit for the kingdom of God."

This Scripture refers to a plow in a field, not a snowplow. I was confused; it didn't make sense to me.

I opened the Bible I had in the car and read a few verses before. Luke 9:57–62 (ESV) says,

> As they were going along the road, someone said to him, "I will follow you wherever you go." And Jesus said to him, "Foxes have holes, and birds of the air have nests, but the Son of Man has nowhere to lay his head." To another, he said, "Follow me." But he said, "Lord, let me first go and bury my father." And Jesus said to him, "Leave the dead to bury their own dead. But as for you, go and proclaim the kingdom of God." Yet another said, "I will follow you, Lord, but let me first say farewell to those at my home." Jesus said to him, "No one who puts his hand to the plow and looks back is fit for the kingdom of God."

God interrupted me while I was sitting in line at a bank drive-through. He had placed me strategically and orchestrated the cars, snowplow, and snow drifting. I believe that God speaks through everyday moments. I know he wants to guide, teach, and encourage us. I believe that if I hadn't noticed the truck, God would have spoken to me at another time, in another way. But he got my attention and delivered a biblical truth that he wanted me to dig further into during a challenging time.

I needed the reminder. I was unemployed through no fault of my own, and it was so frustrating. The woman whom I worked for had just passed away. I had been with her for eight years. The timing couldn't have been worse because my husband just got laid off. I was grateful for my savings, but I felt anxious and afraid. My life felt like it was falling apart.

Jesus has asked me to follow him, and I must remember that this means I can't put anything else before him, not even things that seem necessary or good. He beckons me to go and proclaim the kingdom of God. I must be willing to live as he directs me because this life is no longer my own. My life is his.

God reminded me that there are no exceptions. If I choose to follow him, I cannot look back. He expects me to move forward. He tells me that he is making a way for me, even if it seems like what he is doing is as crazy as driving backward in heavy traffic. He is God, and he will do things his way. He can see what I cannot see from my vantage point, just as the snowplow driver could see the snow that had drifted onto the road when I couldn't. What he was doing made no sense to me until I could see that snow on the plow as it was cleared away.

God might seem like he is driving backward. Our situation might seem out of control. But I know God's character and believe what he does is for my good.

To be certain I had learned this lesson, God asked me to follow him into the unknown for three full months of drastic change. Ninety days is a long time to commit to, but this was where I would show him I was ready to trust him. In the next chapter you will read about the season that produced in me a tenacious kind of trust. God asked me to change everything. It was the scariest thing I have ever done!

Chapter Nine

Digging A Well, Ninety Days of Healthy Living

———— • O • ————

Question: Do you think God might have a good plan for how you could change?

————o-o-o————

With a rush of immeasurable force, I was bowled over by fear and pain. There was so much pain! I was driving in my car when I noticed a tightness in my chest. Once I stopped at a red light, I reached to check my pulse. The first two fingers of my right hand searched for the gland on the side of my neck under the Burberry plaid scarf tied loosely to keep me warm. My breath billowed through my quivering lips, a cloud of life disappearing as fast as it appeared in the frosty air around me. The strength and velocity of the beat of my heart was horrifying. I quickly pulled my hand away in disbelief.

It reminded me of the time my doctor told me I had Graves' disease; it felt like my heart could leap out of my chest and onto the floor. "No," I whispered, "Not again, God. Please, not again!" I was at my limit, I thought, as the light turned green. I pressed the accelerator, my hand trembling on the steering wheel. "Help me, God!" I yelled, startling even myself. I headed home, knowing I couldn't face the grocery store.

I had promised myself that I would go, no matter what. "I failed again," I mumbled as I unlocked my front door and started up the stairs. Inside my house, it was dark. No one was home but my sweet dog, Eva. I flopped onto the couch, and she jumped up to kiss my face. As Eva curled into a ball on my lap, I leaned back and closed my eyes. "You are going to have to heal me, God," I said, exerting the last bit of energy I could muster. "I need help." I drifted off to sleep.

I woke to a deep, rich voice that sounded like it was coming from a speaker inside my head. The beautiful tone echoed as if someone was talking with a microphone. It was audible, but it felt like it only to me. "Who is that?" I thought as I began to rouse myself awake.

Then, in an instant, I knew it was God. I heard God say, "Dig a well for ninety days."

"What?" I wondered what that meant.

As I prayed and listened, I began to hear more. Grabbing a pen and paper, I scribbled wildly. "The well will be deep," he said. "The well not only refers to reaching the living water inside you, but it is a picture of the wellness I want you to have." God's Holy Spirit guided me as I tried to keep up with writing the words I heard. The pen felt like it was moving in my hand by itself. I was lost in the flow of the moment. I allowed my hand to write without reading, trusting the words because I trusted God at that moment more than I ever had.

"I love you too much to allow you to stay this way, child," God continued. "You are mine, and there is healing for you." The voice began to quiet, and I let the pen go from my hand.

God was challenging me to live differently. It was bizarre to me that he told me an amount of time. I wondered why he said ninety days as I pulled my feet up from the floor onto the couch. I began to read what I had written. So many details were on the page. I was supposed to eat unprocessed foods such as chicken, fish, vegetables, fruit, and grains. There was a mandate to drink water all day and night. And there was an entire section about spending time with God in new ways. He wanted me to do more listening, believing, and obeying his direction. I was to dig a well for healthy living, which appeared to begin with recognizing and trusting his voice.

Ninety days was a long time. The first time I tried to do a Daniel fast with my church, I had trouble, and that was only for twenty-one days. The Daniel fast didn't include chicken or fish, but it did require abstaining from processed foods, additives, sweeteners, and caffeine. The purpose of that fast was less about food and more about spiritual devotion. It was based on the story of Daniel in the Bible, where Daniel chose God over the rich foods offered to him by the Babylonians who had captured him. The royal food they offered him was the best. But God proved that he could sustain Daniel on any diet as long Daniel's devotion was to God only. It has since become a Christian practice to intentionally focus on God by changing eating habits, relying less on food, and learning to rely more on him as in any biblical fast.

Why did I believe I could change for ninety days if I struggled with twenty-one days? God's plan sounded too simple to work, but I answered yes and would try to stick to what I promised him, determined to follow his guidance.

Those ninety days became a time of transformation and renewal. As I prayed and listened, I began to hear more details from God. He was challenging me to live a new way. In addition to the physical changes, he called me to prolonged obedience. Changing my daily habits for a long time meant creating a new lifestyle, a testament to the power of faith and obedience.

When I started, it seemed impossible, but God gave me a strategy. As I began to eat healthier food, I noticed after a while that I didn't miss food that was more about comfort than nutrition. I felt nourished by the unprocessed foods I was consuming. Drinking more water felt great. It was as if I had been dehydrated my entire life and somehow had never known it.

Spending more time with God was complicated. I already got up at five o'clock in the morning to start my day with him. What I found myself doing, though, was being open to experiencing God in new and unexpected ways all day long. I began to see and hear him in everyday moments. He spoke in his creation, my environment, and even the thorny people and circumstances around me. I started to recognize him everywhere. I spent a lot more time listening. Before that, I didn't realize how often I was doing the talking, the deciding, or the worrying. There was a lightness and a peace in my heart when I sat expectant to hear God. I felt excited and hopeful as I waited to hear what God had to show me.

I shed over thirty pounds and three dress sizes that year. Before that, I had been diagnosed with three autoimmune diseases. My doctors told me I had Graves' disease, fibromyalgia, and chronic fatigue syndrome. Each new diagnosis had added unwanted weight gain, fatigue, and brain fog to my life. And then menopause began.

When I was younger, I could wear anything and eat anything I wanted, and I usually did both. But after gaining so much weight, I felt lost, depressed, and unlovable. I had tried everything I could think of to lose weight, but nothing seemed to work. Even climbing the stairs in my home became a challenge.

As the months passed, my body began to change. I lost weight, and my hair and skin started to look healthier, too. It took losing two dress sizes before others seemed to notice what was happening on the outside. When they inquired, it allowed me to tell them what was happening inside. The transformation was a testament to God's love and power, giving me a new avenue to speak about my relationship with him.

God had more in store for me. I had been standing at a crossroads; to the left was my current life, but to the right was the change God told me I would need for the next season. As I stood there and intentionally chose to follow his direction, something that had always had a stronghold over me broke—my anxious need to be in control. I needed to be in charge for years because of what others had done to me. It was fear mixed with pride, plain and simple, but I had convinced myself I was the only one I could trust. I didn't believe that anymore. God proved he was trustworthy repeatedly. I stepped out from under the heavy weight of fear, and with that first step into the unknown, I left it behind.

I was already free when I believed God over my voice and the enemy's lies; I just hadn't seen it yet. I had lost all the weight in the spiritual realm before I saw the results in the physical world. The weight loss happened as soon as I chose to honestly believe that God could help me do what had been impossible for me to do on my own. This sense of freedom was empowering and liberating.

Having doctors tell me that I had these illnesses with symptoms and effects restricted my belief that God could do anything to help me. It took obedience to his plan and trusting his character to break free from what had enslaved me.

I continue to make healthy choices. A change in my heart needed to happen before the change in my body could follow. I have been through some challenging things. I am learning to be God's daughter first, realizing everything else falls into its rightful place from there. I have learned the value of trusting God and his plans. Not only did God have a plan for me to get healthier, but this was preparation for what would come next.

About a month into this lifestyle change, a friend from church contacted me. She said I needed to meet her friend, Melody. I agreed, and we met for breakfast. As it turned out, I did need to meet her! Melody was having a women's event, and by the time we finished breakfast, I agreed to pray about sharing my testimony at her event.

When I first started the ninety days of digging a well, God asked me to write my full testimony down and to be ready to share it. I was learning to be more obedient, so I wrote it down. I was curious to know if I would ever share what I wrote with anyone else.

I have noticed that is how God speaks to me, one task at a time. He gives me chances to follow him, join him in unfamiliar places, and do new things. "Behold, I am doing something new; now it springs forth, do you not perceive it? I will make a way in the wilderness and rivers in the desert," I heard God say. I felt like I had read that before and looked in the Bible and found the words in the book of Isaiah (43:19).

I decided to speak at the event, and when I did, I discovered that the date scheduled was the first day after my ninety days of wellness. It was a sign I was on the right path, an affirmation that I had heard God correctly. This brought me a profound sense of fulfillment and a hopeful anticipation for what would come.

When I arrived at the venue, one of my friends pointed to a stone well on the edge of the property. I told her what God said about digging a well for ninety days. I posed for a picture next to it, which I still have sitting in my bedroom in a gold-specked frame.

Not only did the well stand for what God had asked of me, but when I asked God how he wanted me to share my story, he suggested I use the story of the woman at the well from the book of John. Amazingly, I had never thought of myself being represented in this story, but it was the perfect one to use because I had two husbands before I met Jesus. I was the woman at the well.

Melody and I have become friends. I love to talk and to pray with her. She is a great encouragement. It feels impossible to think we haven't always known each other. It's crazier yet that we met in such a clandestine way. I will be forever grateful that my friend Meenu heard God clearly and was obedient to connect us.

God has a plan. I now see my life from his perspective. These seasons I live through are just a blip along his timeline. Today is a mist and will be gone before I notice. He had been leading me right here, to this moment, all along.

For example, years ago, I heard God ask me to start a blog. "Be vulnerable," he said. I agreed naively, and a blog was born. Shortly after I began writing, my world felt like it started to fall apart, but it was falling into place. I continued to be transparent as I had promised. Because of my obedience, I chronicled the most miraculous times.

Since then, God has guided and directed my steps, and I have been willing to venture onto his path for me. Authoring books and podcasting have been added to the list of things I couldn't have done without God. I am eager to do what he says is best for me; even though I don't always know what is coming, I can trust the One asking me to step out into something new. One step led to another until, before I knew it, I had settled into God's plans for my life.

My story carries his story. Every time I write, I get to share how amazing he is. I am incredibly grateful for the people who want to hear about my God's heart and how he loves his children.

There is a story in the Bible that describes God's love for us better than I ever could, so I want to share it with you. It shows the incredible power of our adoption into God's family.

In this story Jesus takes the time to speak truth over a woman with no name. She doesn't know who she is because she doesn't know whose she is! Not only does Jesus heal her physical needs, but more importantly, he heals her heart by reminding her who she is.

This is what I needed too. My physical and emotional healing meant nothing until I was reminded of who God created me to be. Turn the page with me and see the intentional beauty of how God loves every one of his children.

Chapter Ten

Daughter

—————— • ○ • ——————

Question: What are your thoughts about Jesus?

————o-o-o————

The rushing crowd pressed in on her. "Help," she cried out, but no one heard her above the clamor. The murmur of voices built to a crescendo, piercing her ears and making her stop. "I can't do it," she whispered, crossing her arms in front of her chest to hug herself. She hadn't hugged another person in twelve years. Just then, with a strength that was not her own, she threw her arms down and reached forward, slowly crouching down near the ground. The dust from the footsteps around her enveloped her face. She reached through the sea of bodies with her eyes fixed firmly on him, on Jesus. She needed to touch Jesus. Even if she only got to touch the hem of his garment, she knew he could heal her.

With the last bit of hope she could muster, a faith that made no sense rose in her spirit. Then, this brave woman lurched forward and stretched her arm as far as it could go. The pain from kneeling on the stony ground was excruciating. Her knees began to bleed. That was nothing new, she thought, wiping the blood away and watching it smear onto her clothing. She had been bleeding for twelve years.

"He can and he will," she shouted, but no one could hear her. Jesus was walking through the crowd to go to Jairus' house with the disciples all around him. When this woman on the ground finally saw his face, she knew everything they said about him was true. She believed it. When all hope was gone, when nothing else had worked, somehow, she had the faith to try one last time.

Her fingers were rough and dirty from the ground. When they touched the tassels on the hem of Christ's garment, this woman felt a warm surge of energy pass through her body. She pulled back her hand and sat on the ground while people continued to walk around her as if she wasn't there.

"It stopped," she whispered, reaching down to softly place her hand over her belly. "I am not bleeding," she exclaimed a little louder. She was invisible to the people bustling past her, but she didn't care anymore. Jesus had healed her.

In awe and gratitude, the woman cried softly. Her salty tears mixed with the dust in the air and made bold streaks down her face.

"Who touched me?" Jesus said loudly, stopping in the crowd. He knew power had gone out from him.

"Master, the people are crowding and pressing against you," Peter replied, not realizing what had happened.

"Power went out from me." Jesus turned to look into the sea of people around him.

I found myself leaning in, utterly drawn to this woman I was reading about in the Bible. She was called the woman with an issue of blood. The people in the crowd were her neighbors; they knew her, but no longer knew her name because she had been sick for so long. She endured the pain and loneliness of her infirmity for twelve long years. It wasn't her fault. She had nothing to do with the illness that caused her to bleed, but under the Levitical law of her day, any woman with a bloody discharge was considered unclean. Because of this, she was cut off from the life she had once known.

Desperate and alone, this woman had reached out to every physician. They couldn't heal her. Eventually, after spending everything she had, she succumbed to the idea that she would be alone forever.

I wonder how long it took her to cry out to God. Or did she blame God at first like I had? I was sick too, and none of the doctors I saw could offer me healing. The autoimmune diseases I had most likely were a result of the trauma my poor little body endured as a child. Having PTSD from unresolved sexual and emotional trauma has been linked to autoimmune disease. Stress releases hormones such as cortisol, which can weaken the immune system.

Renowned retired physician and author Dr. Gabor Maté, who specializes in the relationship between the mind and body, says, "When you shut down emotion, you are also affecting your immune system and your nervous system. So, the repression of emotion, which is a survival strategy, then becomes a source of physiological illness later." In simple terms, if you push down your emotions, your body will express them as symptoms.

All those years of living in a state of hypervigilance, walking through my life in a constant fight-or-flight reaction, had wreaked havoc on my body.

I remember the days when I could barely talk on the phone without tiring. The flashbacks of conversations with my kids that I can only describe as feeling like I wasn't in the room with them but viewing them through a movie camera instead. Those memories haunted me. The reality of being disconnected from everyone I loved was sinister. I shed more tears those days than any other time in my life. I was certain I would never feel "normal" again.

I closed my eyes for a moment and, breathing in deeply, I prayed, "God why do I feel angry right now?" A shaft of golden light came through my bedroom window and landed on the pages of my Bible. One word shone brightly, as if God were putting a heavenly spotlight on it just for me. The word "daughter" glowed with life. I took another deep breath, curious and expectant in the moment. "What about daughter is so important?" I asked God. My dog, Molly, looked at me from the bed as if I were crazy talking to no one, but I was talking to God. She just couldn't see him. "I don't understand how that's an answer," I said challenging him as if he were seated right next to me, because he was with me. I knew it. His presence began to affect the atmosphere. I looked down at the page of my Bible and continued to read.

"The people in the crowd knew this bleeding woman by what had happened to her," I thought as I read on. I don't think she knew her name either. God showed me that her identity had been overridden by what had happened to her, just like me.

"Wow." A lightbulb switched on in my mind. "Oh, I am like this woman," I responded again as if God were sitting across from me. No one knew who I was anymore either. I pursed my lips together and began to feel sorry for myself. "But everyone knows what's wrong with me."

I felt a camaraderie with her. This woman would get me. I would get her too. It had been so long since I felt understood, since I felt seen. No one saw me. I could be in a crowd and no one could see my pain. But God ... God saw me. He showed me something new. In this story, Jesus called the woman out of the crowd, out of her false identity. He gave her a name. He called her "daughter."

This was not just a term of endearment, but a declaration of her belonging. Jesus wanted her to know that she was part of his family. She was the daughter of the King!

Can you imagine what it would be like if everyone knew you for what you were going through? "Oh, there's the woman who's divorced. There's the woman who had a miscarriage. There's the woman who has an addiction. There's the woman with cancer. There's the woman with mental health issues. There's the woman who is overweight." The list goes on and on and on! But just like this woman in the Bible, we are not defined by our struggles or circumstances. God loves us. God sees us. God calls us family. Our identity is his child.

People do the same thing today; they find out what you're struggling with, and that's the name they call you by. It's the opposite of what's supposed to happen in the church, but Jesus calls her daughter, he calls you daughter, and he calls me daughter, having the compassion to remind us of who we are in him.

Jesus shows her compassion. He joins her in her struggle instead of leaving her alone and nameless in the crowd. After spending years shut off from family and friends by my season of suffering, I had forgotten who I was. I often defined my identity by my roles as a parent, employee, wife, or friend. I was depressed. I was tired. I felt numb.

Can you imagine being unable to hug anyone for twelve years? During the pandemic, I couldn't hug my daughter or speak to her without being six feet away with a mask on because I chose to live with my parents to care for them. That time was excruciating, but I was still able to hug my son, who lived with me. I was able to hug my parents too. I can't fathom not touching another person for that many years. Can you?

It says in the book of Matthew 9:20–22 (my paraphrase) that the woman who had been subject to bleeding for twelve years touched the hem of Christ's garment, saying, "If only I touch the hem of his garment I will be healed."

Jesus turned and saw her. "Take heart, daughter. Your faith has healed you." Immediately, she stopped bleeding. This passage is significant because it illustrates the power of faith and the transformative nature of Jesus' healing.

The word the Bible chooses to use in this passage for "hem" means fringe, tassel, or the border of a garment. In Numbers 15:38–39 (NKJV), God gave a command that makes this detail significant. It says, "Speak to the children of Israel: Tell them to make tassels on the corners of their garments throughout their generations, and to put a blue thread in the tassels of the corners. And you shall have the tassel, that you may look upon it and remember all the commandments of the LORD and do them." Men sewed these tassels on the mantle they wore, a long rectangular cloth draping down over the body with four corners at the bottom. The Israelites were to attach tassels to the four corners of their garment.

When the woman with the issue of blood touched the hem of Jesus' garment, she would have touched one of the tassels. We must recognize the deep and significant meaning of the place where this woman reached out to touch Jesus. The hem and tassels on Jesus' garment were substantial. They told us who people were at that time. These items would show a person's status in society. The hem symbolized the owner's identity and authority.

Anyone who wrote legal contracts at that time wrote them on clay tablets, and they were signed by pressing the corner of one's hem into the clay. In 1 Samuel 24:3–5, David encounters Saul in a cave, and instead of killing Saul, he cuts off part of the hem of his garment. David felt great remorse because, even though he didn't kill King Saul as he could have, cutting his hem meant assaulting his authority to reign. Tassels were a sign of nobility. Kings and princes wore them.

The woman, considered impure and shunned by society, dared to touch the hem of Christ's garment. At that moment, power flowed from him, and her bleeding ceased. Jesus, calling out into the crowd, asked, "Who touched me?" She had touched his identity and authority where the tassels were, the holiest part of his garment. Jesus' purity was so great that instead of becoming defiled by her touch, he transformed her impurity with his identity. This is the transformative power of Jesus, the hope that even the most impure can be made pure. The hope I cling to for myself.

Jesus didn't call out because he didn't know who touched him. He knew. Jesus did not call out because he didn't know who she was. He did. Jesus called her out of the crowd because he wanted *her* to know who she was.

Jesus could have just healed her and moved on. He could have kept walking. He was on the way to healing another daughter, the only child of a synagogue leader named Jairus. While Jesus was taking the time to intentionally interact with the hemorrhaging woman, people came from Jairus' house to tell him the little girl had died.

For Jairus, all hope had died with his daughter, just as the woman with the issue of blood had lost hope of ever being healed … but God! God had a different plan. Jesus went to Jairus' home anyway. He told him not to be afraid but to believe in him. Jesus took the little girl by the hand and said, "Talitha koum," which means "Little girl, I say to you, get up!" In response, the girl immediately stood up and started walking around. She was twelve years old.

Twelve years is mentioned in both these stories we find intertwined in the gospels. The woman had been bleeding since

Jairus' little girl was born. Twelve is a significant number for the Jewish people. By using it, God emphasizes the value, worth, identity, and deliberate choice of loving these two daughters.

Jesus could have continued to where he was going, but it was essential for him to stop and be intentional. He wanted this daughter to know her worth!

I think this story is in the Bible because the woman with the issue of blood represents so many of us. Jesus wanted each one of us to know that no matter what we struggle with and no matter how many years we've been struggling, even if no worldly thing has helped us, even if we have spent all our time and money and exhausted all our hope, Jesus has the power to heal us. We need only reach out our hand in faith.

We know by faith that the identity of God is a good Father, and our identity is his child. From this intimate place we can experience a relationship with God instead of only knowing his law and regulations. Only through the power of this relationship can we experience resurrected life and healing.

God goes into detail to name the women in Jesus' genealogy. In that time women were not looked at with importance, but God sees his daughters as valuable. The women named are Tamar, Rahab, Ruth, Bathsheba, and Mary. In a time when women were not allowed to take part in legal matters, Jesus' lineage provided a permanent record of these women. Each life had its struggle, an intricate story of doubt and healing. God included them in Jesus' genealogy so we could find ourselves there too. They were part of his family, and so are we.

Our families may have generations of brokenness. We all come from some sort of dysfunction, but in Christ, there is healing. Jesus can resurrect our families, and we can start a new family line—if we only we stretch out our hand towards him in faith.

Christ's genealogy mentions five women. Four of them were grandmothers, and one was Christ's mother. In the example of the four grandmothers, we see Tamar, who was manipulative, having to sexualize a situation to regain a broken promise. Next is Ruth, a noble and faithful foreign woman the Israelites did not accept. She chose family and God over her culture. Then we have Rahab, who was a prostitute who helped the Israelite spies. She believed in her heart that God was the one true God. Bathsheba was innocently taking a bath when the king coerced her into adultery. At that time, she couldn't say no. Last, we have Mary, Jesus' mother, a virgin who loved God in her heart, and even though she was confused and scared, she believed the words the angel spoke to her.

The Bible included these ladies to show the different things women deal with in a society that doesn't acknowledge them equally. I think God is saying that he can take the lineage and ancestry in the genealogy of brokenness in our past and bring it to a place that is pure and usable through Jesus. I think it's beautiful that Jesus' genealogy includes these women.

God wants us to know that we can live differently no matter our background or what our parents or grandparents did. There is no deed that cannot be redeemed through God's Son and made holy and pure again.

The encouragement and hope deeply woven into these stories are for you today, no matter what struggle you are facing or how long it's been. You are a child of the King. You are his family. You can be healed. You need only reach out to him in faith.

Both Jesus and Jairus called someone daughter. Both cherished them. By society's standards, neither of them should be making a public spectacle over these women the culture saw as "unimportant ones." But they didn't care about rules; they cared about their families. Their daughters were more important to them than what society had to say.

My lack of knowledge about my identity had secluded me too. I spent years shut off and alone, ostracized by the healthy people living all around me. When I dared to believe that Jesus was my way to receive healing, I stretched out my hand towards him. I cried out his name. He answered, calling me daughter.

Once God had restored my identity, he had plans to resurrect the places in my life that still appeared dead to me. In God's hands anything is possible. He was asking me to stretch my faith wide to embrace the reality that he could bring me fully back to life. The real question was, did I believe him? In the next chapter I share the miraculous ways God challenged my faith. It seems whenever I think I am done healing, God has more for me.

Chapter Eleven

In the Valley of the Dry Bones

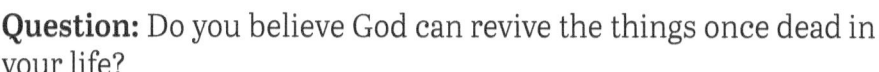

Question: Do you believe God can revive the things once dead in your life?

———o-o-o———

I closed my eyes and leaned back on my couch, pulling the sheepskin blanket from my legs up around my shoulders. Colors began to form in my mind. With my eyes still closed, the blackness came into clear focus. Lush green mountains towered above the valley in the distance. *Trickle, trickle, trickle, splash, gurgle.* Water flowed beyond the valley floor as it made its way over the rocks and pebbles. The stream evoked an instant feeling of peace. The valley itself was dry and desolate. As I surveyed the land before me, in my mind's eye, it was an endless expanse of dusty earth, a deep burnt umber, hot and barren.

"What are you showing me, God?" I continued to be drawn into the vision. A startling sound in the distance broke through, a heavy metal clanging; iron upon iron reverberated around me. The echoes of swords warring against each other created fiery sparks from the clashes.

"This is where the battle was fought, my child."

I walked towards the mountains and into the vast open expanse. "What is that in the distance?" I squinted to see what it could be. I lifted my hand across my brow to shield my eyes from the light above. I remember thinking the light wasn't from the sun but from God himself, but I never looked up to see. It was a feeling in my heart. My attention was fixed on the large piles of whatever I saw in the distance.

The dust from the ground billowed up and hung like storm clouds every time I took a step. "Are those skeletons?" I gasped loudly, squinting harder. I was almost up to the first mound of them. "Those are bones, God! Where am I? Where are you taking me?" I stopped walking to take a deep breath.

This valley scene was so deep in my heart that if I drew a heart like a child does, it would be at the very bottom point, at that sharp little place where the two soft, rounded halves meet—a barren valley filled with dry bones.

I was now standing in front of piles of bones. As far as the eye could see, they were strewn across the valley floor like a giant toddler had thrown them there.

"Why are these here, God?" I stood squarely, careful not to step on the bones.

"These are the remains," God answered.

"The remains of what?"

"Of your battles. You haven't looked at them in years, but these bones are the remnants of the wars that were fought in you. You are standing in the valley of your past," God said, his voice beginning to boom and crash. It sounded like rushing water.

"Why am I here?"

"For healing," he answered.

I wondered how standing all alone surrounded by death and bones was going to heal me. I bent down to a squatting position and reached to touch the bony hand in front of me. It was strangely soothing. As I ran my finger across the top of the splintered bone, God asked me, "Amanda, can these bones live?"

"No," I answered, being honest with myself about my sordid past. "No God, they can't live." Earlier that morning I had read about a valley of dry bones in the Bible. God began to show me this in my life.

I hadn't looked at those things for years. They were dead and dry—I couldn't even recognize these skeletons anymore. I left them there to turn to dust.

God asked again, "Amanda, can these things live?"

I should have said, "Only you know, Lord," just like Ezekiel said in the story I had read, but what I have been saying to myself all these years is, "No, no, they are dead. They are dry. They are bones. They can't live!"

The story from chapter thirty-seven of the book of Ezekiel is an incredible one, so unconventional that I may not have believed it possible. The story is about a vision of a prophet of God. His name, Ezekiel, means "God strengthens" in Hebrew.

Ezekiel was among the captives taken to Babylon, an enemy city during the first fall of Jerusalem. He authored the book of Ezekiel while in captivity there. As far as assignments from the Lord go, he got a difficult one. Who wants to hear from a God who allows you to live as a captive, right? But the story doesn't go like that. God had given his chosen people many chances to do the right thing. They never did, despite all his warnings. And like every good parent I know, when his kids didn't listen, he had no choice but to follow through with the consequences of their actions.

God continued to speak and offer his comfort during those years. One day, Ezekiel was taken in a vision to the center of a valley filled with bones.

In the story, Ezekiel says that it was because of God he was there. The Spirit of God brought him to that place and set him in the middle of it. Not on the edge, but directly onto the piles of bones strewn across the valley floor. He recounts that there were a lot of bones, so don't just picture one skeleton; picture piles of them. The Bible says the bones were brittle and dry.

This was most likely the remains of a battle scene. Soldiers fought wars in the valleys at that time. Brave soldiers, fighting for their lives, died instead. These bodies must have sat in the sun decomposing while wild animals came and fed on their flesh. Over time, laying there exposed to the elements, they began to dry out.

The bones snapped underfoot as Ezekiel walked over them. He walked back and forth over the bones as the Lord had commanded him. The shards pushed violently through the thin leather sandals on his feet. Billows of dust rose as he took each painful step. It's strange how something so tiny as a piece of bone can cause so much damage. A splinter shot through the arch of his foot. "Ouch." Ezekiel winced in pain.

"Keep walking," God commanded him. *Snap, clink, snap.* Every step made the bones beneath him rattle and break.

"God, this hurts," he said, knowing he must obey the Lord. Ezekiel stretched his arms out to help keep his balance as he climbed the mountainous pile of bones. "No," he shouted as he slipped and fell face first into the dead bodies. Slowly Ezekiel rolled over, the bones poking deeply into his back. "What do you want from me, Lord?" Blood trickled from his foot onto the stark white bones.

"Can these bones live?" God asked the prophet who lay there limp and exhausted.

"Only you know, Lord." He took a strained breath.

"Speak to the bones and to tell them to hear the word of the Lord," God commanded him.

So, he spoke to the bones. *Rattle, clink.* The scattered bones began to attach to each other, forming complete skeletons. Miraculously, tendons and sinews and flesh covered them. Now, with his face on the ground in worship and awe, Ezekiel heard God give him one last instruction.

"Speak to the breath. Tell my breath to enter the army before you," God commanded. As the prophet followed God's commands and spoke to the bones, the breath entered them, and suddenly they were alive! There stood a battalion of resurrected men. Scripture calls them a vast army.

For weeks before my conversation with God, I kept hearing about skeletons and dry bones. I read devotions that referenced them. I heard little kids singing, "Them bones, them bones, them dry bones, now hear the word of the Lord." I heard worship songs from two contemporary Christian bands with lyrics about these bones. I also came to the actual book of Ezekiel in my daily Bible reading. It seemed imperative that I look at this story in a personal way. So, I did. I prayed and asked God to speak to me through this vision. I didn't ever expect to have one myself.

I had convinced myself that I would have answered the same way Ezekiel did. But when God prompted me to answer him, I could see that I had doubts.

My dry bones, my piles of shame and regret, the stuff that's been underfoot since before I became a Christian, the things I didn't want anyone else to know about—God knew they were there. My sexual exploits. My drinking. My drug use and the words I chose to use instead of truth to avoid dealing with inconvenient situations, my lies. My need to be in control and to manipulate the world and the people around me. Stealing, cheating, cursing, conniving—my ugly heart was on display.

God wanted to transform all of it. He longed to heal me, to speak life, not to scare me or shame me. He wanted to put his breath in me.

He wanted to redeem those places I was so sure were dead.

What if I were to let him take all those things I thought were too broken to fix and speak his truth over them? What if he could change everything? What if I connected with other people who doubted and showed them God transformed me?

God's breath brought death to life in me. I took a black felt tip pen and drew in my journal a picture of a skeleton next to a person fully clothed in flesh. Then, I drew the breath of God entering what was dead, drawing tiny dashes in a circular motion to stand for God's living breath exhaling from the body.

I closed my eyes and listened for God. As I sang the lyrics to a worship song that was playing in the background, I saw my resurrected self as I began to walk away from the valley of bones. I started singing over the image, trusting in the truth that my chains binding me to the dead things of my past were broken in God's presence. I left the valley behind, moving forward with life and breath, reborn and renewed.

As I walked toward the majestic mountains in the distance, a butterfly circled my head. Its fragile wings pushed up and down in the air, pumping softly, lifting it higher. "Wow," I said with the awe and wonder of a little child, "You're beautiful!" Its bright indigo wings glimmered in the sunshine. Golden shocks of light shone on the horizon like giant flashlights from the sky.

"I am new, God; I feel it," I whispered, stretching my arms to each side and tilting my head back. "You did it!" I shouted joyfully as I flapped my new wings and spun in wild toddler circles. A warm, fresh wind blew across my face and filled my lungs all at once. "I am new," I shouted with joy. My lips began to turn upwards at the corners until I was fully smiling. "I am going to be alright. Everything is going to be okay."

After bringing the impossible into reality, God invited me to a time of sifting and rest. I didn't realize how much I needed it. God had plans for my future, but he couldn't let me step into them until my heart was ready. His work in me felt like surgery. Sharp piercing cuts revealing diseased places. Stitches cinching the flesh in place. Time and rest allowed the incisions to heal. As the patient unexpectedly placed on the operating table, I experienced uncertainty and sometimes even fear. With only one step revealed at a time, I had to trust God's plan for me. In the next chapter you will find a perilous, wilderness time God had prepared for me. There was no other way to prepare me for the season to come. God hid me away.

Chapter Twelve
Hidden Away

———————— • O • ————————

Question: Have you ever had a job helping others?

————o-o-o————

"God, I know you asked me to do this, but you didn't tell me there would be a pandemic!" I yelled at the top of my lungs. *Crunch, crunch, crunch.* The all too familiar sound of winter resonated beneath my feet. As I walked away from my house, the icy crystals of frost on the ground glistened rhythmically like blinking stars in the sky at night. The sun shone on them intently between the fleeting clouds. Faster and faster, I walked, trying to get as far away from the house as I could. This is where I went to argue with God.

"I can't take any more of this," I said as my voice shivered and quaked, beginning to crack. I felt the hot and uncontrollable emotions I had tried to push down leap up and out of my mouth. It felt like fire, flames licking, burning everything good up into ash. The weathered wooden bench I put under our maple tree was my spot. I had carefully placed it there as soon as the world began to shut down around us under the never-ending orders of the CDC. "Can't you make coronavirus disappear?"

I stood back up again, nervously pacing across the yard. "Look at this house, God." The farmhouse in front of me looked brilliant. It was whitewashed in the dazzling morning sunlight. Two-foot-thick stone walls stood beneath that plaster and paint. My house was built in the 1600s. "I wonder if they went through a pandemic here before?" I said aloud, placing my hand on my chin and then over my mouth. The warm vapor of my breath swirled through my fingers and spread thinly into the air and then vanished.

I had watched the maple branches that once held green, emerald leaves turn to hues of red and yellow. Each day, their vibrant beauty turned crisp and brown as they let go and fell together, strewn across the ground in a final tribute to autumn. Tilting my head back to look up, all I saw were empty branches rough and grey. *Clap, rattle, squeak.* The branches sounded their alarm, knocking against one another in the wild winter wind. "Brrrr," I said shivering all over. I quickly clutched my collar around my neck. Why does everything have to change, I wondered. Not just the seasons but also people and life too.

This was the house I grew up in. Saying yes to caring for my parents wasn't an easy decision. Coming back was traumatizing. I had made boundaries and gone through healing; why would I want to be susceptible to the ones who wounded me again? The problem was that I clearly heard God tell me it was time to go there. This was his plan.

"It's time to prepare to care for your parents," God said, interrupting a perfectly fine day.

"What?"

"Can't someone else help them," I wondered. But I knew God was asking me to, not just for them but for me, my heart, my growth, and my healing. Yes, I would be my parents' caregiver, but God had plans for more than I could imagine. It was very much like the story of Elijah at the Kerith Ravine.

In 1 Kings 17, before God sent his prophet Elijah to the Kerith Ravine, God told him to declare a drought on the land. Directly after he obeyed God by prophesying about the drought, the word of the Lord came to Elijah. God said, "Depart from here and turn eastward and hide yourself by the brook Kerith, which is east of the Jordan" (vs 3).

I always thought a brook was a tiny running stream, a moving current of water. But when I researched this text, I found the word Kerith is a common English spelling of the Hebrew name Kerit, which means "to cut off." The name also signifies to engrave or carve, typically a gorge or ravine. Elijah had just declared that there would be no more rain. God had shut up the sky. Then the word of the Lord came to Elijah, telling him to leave, to turn, and to hide.

God promised to feed him, give him water, and allow some rest for the next part of his journey. God supplies all our needs. His provision and protection are more than we can do on our own.

It's truly inspiring to realize that, even in the most cut off and secluded places, God can reveal our purpose. He has a plan and a provision for us. We can find purpose and growth in these difficult seasons.

Since we know God had no plans to send any more rain after commanding a drought, that ravine would only stay full of water for a limited time. It was a clock of sorts, a timer for the season at hand. It's important to note that Elijah traveled where God told him to go and stayed where God put him.

He went from a prominent ministry to being hidden away by himself. Ravens fed him bread and meat morning and evening, and he was able to drink from the ravine. Exhausted, Elijah welcomed the rest God gave him in that season. God knew what Elijah needed.

If God sends you to a place of rest, cut off from everything, for your good, it is because he knows you need it.

This season was an on-purpose time for Elijah—a God-given gift. Elijah was exhausted and anxious, afraid of King Ahab; he gladly followed God's lead. He welcomed the rest, the nourishment, and the seclusion. I dare to say he wasn't alone, even though the Scripture doesn't mention God's presence; we know God's character. I am convinced God was with him too.

The ministry God had called Elijah to as a prophet was difficult. God knew this and continued to supply Elijah's needs until the water dried up, which was a predestined time God had created for Elijah to move on.

When I was cut off and hidden away during the pandemic, I had a challenging time. I am a social person. Before that, I was writing, speaking, and connecting with others to share the goodness of God. I didn't understand why I was suddenly cut off and alone. It was a time of deep personal struggle and doubt when I questioned my purpose and felt isolated. I thought I was a failure.

Out in the world, I felt confident. At church, I had gained leadership opportunities. I mentored young ladies in my spare time. I had written books and been in vital ministries. I felt alive, living out my passion and stepping onto new platforms. I felt a calling to speak and write and encourage others, and I was following that call. Then God sent me off to be separated from what I thought was successfully serving him. He asked me to serve quietly in the background with no fanfare and no platform. Bent low to care for my parents' most basic needs, I worked hard and ended my days exhausted.

Without the ability to go out to the store, have lunch with a friend, or even hug my own daughter because I had chosen to help my parents, the pandemic shut me off from everything else I thought was important.

That was the lesson God had for me. Anything done while serving him was valuable. Making food, cutting lawns, cleaning toilets—all were treasure stored up in heaven. Showing restraint and gentleness in the face of dysfunctional outbursts from those I served stretched me and allowed God to mature the fruit of his spirit in my heart.

Humility and tenacity were my constant companions as I pushed through the doubt and disappointment day after day. God himself was yoked with me, walking through it all. He stopped to show me areas I needed to let go of and gave me examples of how to live a life more like Jesus. He showed me the breathtaking beauty of his creation and encouraged me when I needed it most.

At my lowest point, I doubted myself and any purpose I thought I had, and then God showed me the truth behind this verse. Elijah wasn't "hiding." He was "hidden." God had work to do in his life. While Elijah rested, the Lord worked on his heart, replacing fear with confidence in the wonder-working God he served.

I can now see the personal growth and new opportunities God prepared for me. This challenging season was a stepping stone for my next ministry, a testament to God's faithfulness and provision.

Elijah would need this special time of rest to move into his next season. God's plans for him were for a completely different ministry. Elijah was going to perform miracles on God's behalf—miracles! His heart had to be in alignment with God. Like the potter and clay, God worked diligently and lovingly on Elijah. God threw him back onto the wheel to be shaped and perfected for what he would pour into him next.

My seclusion also produced an entirely new ministry. My podcast was a completely new way for me to share my faith and connect with others. This next step for my life only came because of my "Kerith Ravine" season.

God put a clock on my "hidden away" time too. One day, the world opened, and I was released to return to church, in-person small group ministry, women's ministry, speaking, and writing books again.

Looking back at the platforms and audiences God grew for me during the pandemic, I am astounded by how that could happen while I was shut off in an old farmhouse in the middle of nowhere. God gets all the glory. I wouldn't have chosen what he gave me, but it was exactly what I needed.

I get to point to him when I tell the story of his working in my waiting. I don't think I have ever met anyone who liked waiting on God to move. Waiting is lonely and frustrating. But God does his best work while we wait.

I have learned to trust in his plans and timing. When I cannot hear him, I have disciplined myself to stop and remember how good he is. I declare aloud that he is faithful. I stand on his promises as I wait, finding peace in his sovereignty.

When God is silent, he is growing our faith muscles stronger for our next adventure with him. God whispers when the world around us roars. We must learn how to recognize his voice.

God had put a limit on Elijah's time at the ravine, a clock ticking while he lived in a hiding place, and a season's beginning and end were all established by him. The Bible says that when the ravine dried up, God commanded Elijah to go to Zarephath in Sidon and stay there near a widow, whom God had commanded to take care of Elijah. God sent him to a whole new place of provision to minister in an entirely new way.

Elijah met the widow, which began a season of miracles God empowered. We never know what God has for us until we arrive at our next destination. But we do know God will be with us and provide for us.

We go from provision to provision. In each season, God gives us what we need. The more dramatic the transition from season to season, the more dramatic the change in our assignments.

Do you know what season you are in right now? Does it make sense to you? Have you asked God to tell you what comes next? If any of these things are true, then learning your whole story from beginning to the present will help you.

From this new place of understanding, you might assume I felt confident and secure. You would be wrong. Somehow the idea that God had new ministry and purpose for me threw me into a tailspin. I struggled with my sin. More than the struggle was my inability to make sense of my actions. No matter how many times I searched for root causes and set out to heal, I always succumbed to some remnant of my old life.

Do you struggle with your sins and habits too? In the next chapter, I am completely vulnerable so I can connect with you in a deep and real way. Whether we admit our struggles out loud, or in this case, in writing for the whole world to see, all of us wrestle with our dark places.

Chapter Thirteen

Why Did I Do That?

———————— • O • ————————

Question: If I asked you to share a place you struggle with daily, what would that be?

————o-o-o————

The pressure of the tiny suction cups squeezed my heart tightly as they undulated like waves on the sea. As a massive gray tentacle clutched at my skin, I muttered, "I can't breathe." I gasped as I tried to hold onto the last bit of air left in my lungs. "Help!" Tears dropped from my wild, bloodshot eyes. "I am not strong enough; I can't get loose, God," I prayed softly, struggling to free myself from the death grip that entrapped me. The overwhelming pressure closed in fiercely around me, squeezing the air out of my lungs. Suffocating, I opened my mouth for the relief of a fresh breath, but my lungs couldn't expand against the strength of my enemy.

Gasp. Wheeze. Cough, cough. I shot straight upward in the bed like a board and struggled to catch my breath. "What the..." I exclaimed loudly, realizing it had been a dream. "What was that?"

I got up to grab my journal and a pen to recount what I had been through. As I wrote about the dream, I felt the urge to draw the giant squid-like thing that had been trying to devour me. As I sketched the picture onto the page, I realized that thing still had other limbs to grip and kill with.

I closed my eyes and tried to remember the dream. I felt as if I had forgotten something crucial. "Help me remember, God," I whispered, genuinely believing he would. As I lay there, I started to see what I had forgotten. Two other people were struggling in the monster's grip. As I zoomed in to look at their faces, I was horrified—it was my children!

I opened my eyes and looked down at my journal. "Why were we being attacked, Lord?" I was most bothered by not remembering they were being hurt too. I am a terrible mom, I told myself. Just then, I heard God speaking to me in my heart. "The enemy is your sin, child. You think you only hurt yourself when you sin, but that is untrue. Your sin is like that leviathan that held you captive in its tentacles; as it grips your life, it still has many arms left to attack those around you—your family, friends, anyone near to you."

"How does my sin hurt other people?" Flashes of mini-movies filled my mind. As I watched them reel by reel, I started to understand. Everything is connected. What I don't rebuke will have access to my kids. Generational curses don't happen by coincidence. They happen because an agreement opens the door to the enemy. We must disagree and align our lives with Jesus, or generational repercussions will result. So many doors had been flung wide open by my ancestors. No one had stood in the gap to close them.

I felt numb. I had allowed curses in my life. Not just my life but the lives of my children. Being sexually abused, experiencing parental inversion, and living in an unhealthy, codependent, emotionally toxic family system had affected me. The unrepentant sins of others constrained me. Strongholds were set around my tiny little life.

Why then did I not realize that my sinful choices would affect my kids, too? "Help me, God," I cried, knowing he could see every sinful thing in me. God could hear every thought; even so, he loved me. God knew before I was born every sin I would commit, and yet Jesus went to the cross for me. While I was still a sinner, Christ willingly died for me.

I got up and went to the bathroom to get muscle relaxers for my stiff, throbbing neck. Waking up with that nightmare had stressed me out. Talking to God about sin and the thought that I hurt my kids wasn't helping. As I reached into the medicine cabinet, I stopped and stood frozen. "No," I declared loudly, "I do not need them to sleep." I turned to walk away.

The war inside me began to rage again. "Just take it, and before you know it, you won't have to think about any of this. It's late, and you have a big day ahead. Just take the pill." I knew I no longer needed these, but I loved drifting off quickly to sleep. Without the pills, I would most likely lay there for hours. I pivoted abruptly and marched into the bathroom. Pushing down hard and turning the bottle cap with my hand, I popped the pill bottle open and gently tapped a pill into the palm of my other hand. I smacked my open hand against my lips, and the pill fell squarely on the back of my tongue. Gulp. I swallowed it, and there was no going back.

I returned to the bedroom and slid under the warm, blue-patterned comforter. It fell loosely around my body, hugging me gently. I had already drifted off before I turned on my side to settle in for sleep.

The following morning, I was foggy and irritable when I woke. "Get down," I yelled at my dog, who had come close, lovingly sniffing at my face. I hated the way I felt in the morning after taking those pills. "Crap," I yelled as I woke enough to realize I was late for my appointment. "Great, this sucks," I murmured under my breath as if someone else had done something to me.

The truth was I had done this to myself. Just because those pills were prescribed for me didn't mean I had to keep using them if they made me feel this way. The chronic pain I had in my neck and shoulders was real, but I hadn't told the doctor about my addictive tendencies. Anything I use to escape my feelings or forget reality is unhealthy.

On those nights I scroll through Facebook marketplace looking for the perfect antique table I'm being rebellious and avoidant. I try to convince myself that the treasures I put in my Amazon cart will make my life better, but that is only a lie. True, I might enjoy them for a moment, but until I look head-on at the feelings and behaviors I am avoiding, all of it is just prolonged suffering.

The doctor had told me the muscle relaxers weren't addictive. I started taking them after my car accident. It wasn't as if I was taking narcotics. But they were meant for short-term relief. I had been using them for years. How was this any different from the other ways I tried to numb the pain? How was I still struggling with the same need to feel in control?

I chose to stop taking them, and just like when I quit drinking or smoking cigarettes or any of the myriads of illegal drugs I had used to "feel better," it was hard. Therapy taught me that I had to acknowledge, push through, and feel my feelings instead of running away from them. Therapy works if you follow the doctor's suggestions, but I liked my escape hatches.

Wildly depressed off and on throughout my life, I was no stranger to running from reality. Sleep was my best friend, and I know I slept more than I wanted to think about. Life is for living, but the weight and trauma of what had happened to me screamed louder than the truth.

Eventually, I threw the pills away and stopped refilling the prescription. I made it for years this way until the pandemic, when I discovered melatonin gummies. Honestly, I just found new ways to feel in control during that time. But I convinced myself these little cherry-flavored gummies were safe and natural; even kids took them. During the day, I handled many things. Not only was I cut off from the world, but I was living back at home with the dysfunctional relationships of my parents while trying to be their caretaker. I was depressed. It was a struggle.

One day, I ordered melatonin from Amazon and tried it. It was terrific to drift quickly off to sleep. "I will only use these when I need them," I told myself, but I soon started taking them every night. What I didn't know was they had side effects too. Instead of waking up cranky, I found myself sleepy during the day. I also found out they can worsen depression. Taking melatonin can even cause insomnia after using it for a long time.

They were deceptively cute, looking like the best flavor of the candy "Dots" I used to love as a kid. The red ones were my favorite, and these gummies were all red. I wondered how that connection strengthened my belief that these were harmless?

Justifying any escape from reality meant that my life was not good enough. By not turning to God with my feelings and problems, I was saying that God couldn't help me—remnants of the ruins that had become my heart those years before I met Jesus.

Reverting to running from my feelings wasn't helping anyone. One morning, I asked God to help me get healthy in the unexcavated places he was showing me in my heart. How crazy that I had access to my Creator, who loved me as my Father, and still chose to numb myself instead of going directly to him. There were so many ways to escape reality; all I had to do was turn on the TV, open my laptop, or scroll on my phone. Without leaving the house, I could go anywhere, buy anything, and look at anyone however I wanted. We live in a time when leaning into the folly of our twisted thoughts can rapidly root the seeds of sin in the soil of our hearts.

I have grown far too many harvest fields of rebellion and pride. To numb my pain, I have chased every high known to man. But experiencing God's presence is more fulfilling than any of those escapes. How could I trade the reality of his peace and perfect love for a cheap imitation, for a false god? Why was I running from him instead of to him?

I think some part of me believed God would treat me like people have. I couldn't fully believe he would be faithful. He would reject me, use me, and throw me away, too, wouldn't he? Having fallen for the love bombing of more than one narcissist in my life and living on the crumbs of emotionally toxic people over the years, it was clear my heart was broken. I didn't recognize what was best for me. I would have to let God heal me in the places where I still chose to run away.

Being sexually molested as a child had affected me more than I realized. Once I started therapy and learned about setting healthy boundaries, I was in awe I was allowed to do that. It felt like I was doing something wrong when I wanted to protect myself; I learned that it was not only okay but necessary.

I am no expert, but boundaries are primarily formed in childhood. How others treat a child shape how their boundaries are defined. When a child's needs are met and they feel safe and secure, the child develops and understands healthy personal boundaries.

In stark contrast, abuse and trauma in early childhood can rob a child of the feeling of safety and the need to explore their own identity. Any type of abuse—sexual, emotional, or physical—is a boundary invasion. Victims of abuse experience a loss of control over their lives. If they grow up in a home where boundaries are not respected, they become confused, vulnerable, and insecure. Sadly, these children, like me, don't try to defend their rights to individuality because they never learn they have any. In every way, I felt I existed to serve the needs of others.

I was born into a sea of radical dysfunction, and I was drowning. I didn't know I had a voice or that it could roar.

When I consider the ways I sabotaged myself, I wonder if I wasn't trying to die. Was I trying to kill myself? I do recognize that I was deeply depressed. Jesus genuinely healed me, but so much remained hidden below the surface. Weeds and vines ravaged the wheat and flowers of my heart. God couldn't heal what I wouldn't bring willingly to him.

These moments when we think we know better than God keep us in bondage. As I pondered these things, I walked outside to talk with God. Where I live, the weeds and wild vines grow faster than the flowers I plant on purpose. I know that humans invented the term weed. God made everything good, but when creation fell, thorns and thistles choked the plants we tried to cultivate. It works that way in my heart's soil too.

Every plant has a purpose; poison ivy is food for white-tailed deer, black bears, and muskrats. There are so many plants we consider weeds that have good qualities. For example, before the invention of lawns, dandelions were praised for their golden blossoms and lion-toothed leaves as good for food and medicine from God. Gardeners often weeded out the grass to make room for the dandelions. But somewhere in the twentieth century, humans deemed the dandelion a weed.

I can understand why people don't like poison ivy. I am allergic to it. The pulsating sting and itch of its blisters fill me with dread. Poison is in the name for a reason. Those who react to it know to stay as far away as possible. I wonder what Adam named poison ivy before sin entered the garden.

One day I woke up way before my alarm went off. My arm itched and burned with a fierce and familiar feeling. I had gotten poison ivy. I had been careful whenever I weeded and cut down vines, but I needed more focus. Isn't that how things go? You know what to avoid, but as you rush through your day, you act without thinking and get distracted. I am working on learning to be more focused.

The poison ivy must have gone past my glove when I was pulling weeds. I didn't have a long-sleeve shirt, something I should have done to protect myself. But, because I didn't, I got exposed to poison ivy. I didn't see it, but it found a place to land. That's what the weeds in my heart do—the poisonous things and the wild vines. They flourish if I don't get in there with God's Holy Spirit guiding and covering me.

Have you ever tried to get rid of the roots of poison ivy? Poison ivy has little feet that cling onto things so it can climb up high; its stem grows thick, and its roots grow deep. It's one of the hardest things to get rid of.

The poison of sins can affect me if I'm not paying attention. The things I haven't let the Holy Spirit help me uproot are there. I spent more of my life without Jesus than with him, and the soil of my heart still has many wild vines. The roots are all entangled underneath the soil. I need God's help and guidance; only he knows how to help me.

I am a people-pleaser because I grew up in an environment where I learned to think of the feelings of others before my own. I didn't know how to tell them the truth, and I am still working on it. I often look into the eyes of the person in front of me to see what they want my answer to be.

I learned not to say no to people because I didn't want them to be disappointed. I didn't realize that I put myself last every time I put someone else first. God did not intend for me to push my feelings down to please others. He gave me my feelings and emotions to experience a relationship with him.

Every day I sin. I do the things I don't want to do and don't do the things I want to do. I'm not the only one, but that doesn't give me much relief.

Jesus went to the cross with love in his heart for me despite my sin. He made atonement for me by the shedding of his holy blood. Jesus sits at the Father's right hand, interceding on our behalf. His blood covers us. He made a way home.

Today, instead of walking around with my head down in shame, I lift my eyes to look at Jesus. I will use even the things I am ashamed of as a bridge to reach others who are going through the same struggles.

Somehow God always knows when I most need his encouragement. In the next chapter I want to share an intimate experience with you. God met me in my struggle and gave me a new name. He was so personal and loving I will never forget this moment.

Chapter Fourteen
A New Name

———— • O • ————

Question: If I were to ask you what is the most important thing about you, what would it be?

————o-o-o————

My bedroom was dark except for the tiny white desk lamp on my side table. The soft glow of its light radiated warmly into the darkness. I closed my eyes as I lifted my praises to God and started my day focused on him. "Ha-le-lujiah," the word flowed freely across my lips, releasing into the atmosphere around me. I imagined in my mind's eye each syllable as a musical note floating up to the throne of God. I remember thinking every note had an anointed fragrance. Worship, my genuine worship, was a pleasing aroma to God.

That morning, I had been struggling with generational sin. I was determined to bring my struggles straight to God. While my eyes were still closed, I saw my hands holding sharp, heavy rocks. On these rocks, I saw words painted in thick, black brush strokes. As I read them, I realized they were the same things I had been talking to God about. Anger. Control. Pride. Idolatry. Seeing the words painted in stark black, wet and dripping on the bright white stones, made me shrink back and gasp.

As I looked down and felt their weight in my hands, I realized the rocks had chains attached to them. I could also see those chains had metal handcuffs on the other end. And the cuffs were locked tightly around my wrists.

As I continued to worship, I felt God ask me to let them go. If I would let them go, he would take them, he told me. "Why is this so hard?" I whispered, my hands still clutching the rocks. "They are heavy, and they're cutting me," I cried. "Take them, God. Take them from me."

"You must give them to me, my child." Slowly, I opened my hands to reveal their cuts and scars. With open palms turned upward, I tilted my hands in towards each other, and the stones rolled off them, falling into a deep chasm below me. As they disappeared from my sight, the chains that had been clasped around my wrists broke. The shackles came off!

Deep crimson slashes on my hands closed and healed right before my eyes, replaced by fresh, new skin. I pulled my hands closer to look at them, intently inspecting them in awe. All the wounds had disappeared. Then I saw a hand, which, in my heart, I somehow understood was Jesus' hand. Jesus reached out to me, holding a smooth white stone. It was slightly out of focus, but I could see it in his scarred hand. The piercing that bore straight through his palm cradled the stone.

I knew this was the white stone referred to in the Bible. In the book of Revelation 2:17 (NASB), it says, "To the one who overcomes, I will give some of the hidden manna, and I will give him a white stone, and a new name written on the stone that no one knows except the one who receives it."

Suddenly, my mind flashed back to a memory from years ago when I heard God call me a new name. I was at a retreat in the Pennsylvania mountains. Having woken early, I grabbed my leather-bound journal and favorite pen to sit outside by the lake. The sun rose, resplendent and warm. The way it shone on the gentle capillary waves filled me with wonder. The sparkling movement was melodious. "How do you do it, God?" I quietly asked. My voice rustled through the trees along with the morning breeze. The woods around me were alive with the sounds of animals waking to a new day.

"Lily," I heard suddenly from behind me. Startled, I jumped to my feet and turned, looking in every direction, but no one was there. "Lily, my dear one, I love you," I heard the voice continue.

The deep, rich tone enveloped me with a peace I had never felt before.

If there was ever a time I think I heard the audible voice of God, this was it. Instead of feeling anxious or afraid while alone in the morning mist, I felt a soft and genuine love fall gently around my shoulders, covering me like a warm shawl. I felt its weight and comfort as it lingered like a mantle of God's tangible presence. I crossed my hands in front of my chest, fully taking in the incredible moment. Breathing deeply through my nose, I smelled the sweetness of honeysuckle. "Mmmmmmm, just like when I was little." My words echoed into the forest air.

When I opened my eyes, I scanned the sparkling water before me, then picked up my pen and opened my journal to write. "Lily. He called me Lily." I knew this was a moment I would want to remember forever. Even though I didn't fully understand what was happening, this was a defining moment in my relationship with my heavenly Father. Over the years, God has continued to use this name for me. Each time, it fills me with exuberant joy.

Realizing the white stone I saw was just for me, I expected to see "Lily" engraved on it when it came into focus. As I was thinking, "Lily," I heard a voice say instead, "Rose."

I recoiled in utter confusion. "That's not the name you gave me, God. You gave me the name Lily." For the first time, I doubted that any of this was true.

I sat down and turned off the music. Opening my journal, I began to write. What if I had been making everything up, I wondered. But, as I started to write, God kindly and gently reminded me the other things he had shared with me about the name Lily. My birth flower was the lily of the valley, and it means "return to happiness." I had a crisp memory of toddler me bending down to jingle the lovely ivory bell-like flowers that bloomed along our fence line at my childhood home. I can still smell the captivating, sweet aroma. It evoked pure, innocent joy.

Still smiling from the thoughts of that moment, I decided to look up the biblical meaning of Lily, which is "purity and innocence." I exhaled. "Wow, that is exactly how I felt in that memory, God. Thank you for those memories. Thank you for letting me keep them," I whispered, as tears filled my eyes. I did have some good experiences when I was little, I thought to myself. God was there, after all.

Journaling again, I wondered, "What if when I dropped those stones, Jesus restored me to purity and innocence in those areas of my life?" The thought was exhilarating. I felt like anything was possible.

Next, I looked up the biblical meaning of Rose. A rose symbolizes the resurrection and the blood of Jesus Christ. "No way, God!" I blurted out. When you put the words together, they drew a picture of what I saw happening. I let go of sin, and God resurrected me in those areas through the blood of Jesus. "You're amazing, God," I said, holding my hand over my heart.

Then I looked up the Hebrew word for Lily, because Hebrew was the language used to write the Old Testament. Our names have meanings that are part of the story. It is a challenge to explain how my mind works when I find myself in "investigation mode," as I call it. I am a digger. I ask many questions when I talk to God and look up meanings of words, facts about the time and culture, and the many ways God's creation grows, lives, and works.

Lily in Hebrew was *Shoshana*. I decided to look up what Rose meant in Hebrew as well, still hoping that I could more clearly understand what God was saying to me. While I was looking things up, I wondered why I had never seen the name on the stone Jesus was holding out to me in my vision. Pushing the question aside, I looked up the meaning of Rose next. The answer was unbelievable! The Hebrew meaning of Rose was the same word as for Lily—it was *Shoshana*!

"What?" I shouted. I fell to the floor on my knees, crying. "God, this is impossible! How could two different flowers have the same Hebrew name?" My body felt heavy, and I scooted from my knees to plant my face flat on the floor. Lying prostrate, I whispered my confusion in short staccato sentences to God. My words were muffled by the velvety fibers of the oriental rug I was talking into. I stretched my arms out to the side of my body and turned my head. With a deep cleansing breath, I asked God again. "God, please tell me how this is possible. Is that you? This must be you. You are the only one who could show me this. No one can speak like you do. I believe. Lord, I believe you." I rolled over onto my back. "Two different flowers aren't called the same thing in any language, God. Two names' meanings placed together don't create a sentence of transformation unless you are the one who is speaking." God had declared my purity and innocence through the resurrection blood of Jesus Christ in just two words!

"*Shoshana*," I whispered, enchanted by its sound. "It's my new name, isn't it, Father?" I asked him, already knowing in my heart the answer was yes.

"That's what you wrote on the white stone, God," I shouted, smiling from ear to ear. Jumping up, I bolted from the floor with my arms raised in praise as the sun shone through the window, landing directly onto my chest. Full of wonder and expectant for miracles, I continued, "All that time, you had only told me part of it, but now I know it all, God. Thank you, Father. Praise you, Lord. I praise you, God. Thank you for being so wonderful to me!" I sang with exuberance. "Hello, my name is Shoshana," I chirped like a sweet little girl. Everything about it felt right. "My name is Shoshana," I whispered to God gleefully. "You heard me. You are transforming me. You love me." I believed it all.

These are the moments when the stories I read in the Bible apply to my life too. God had added depth and meaning to our relationship like a colorful gel overlay. My Father had a unique name for me. One that made me feel chosen, wanted, and loved because I was the apple of his eye. Oh, to feel love like that! It made me want to skip and dance. I began to twirl and spin, clothed in the dazzling sunlight beaming through the window. I was alive, fully and wonderfully alive!

So you better understand me, I didn't just look these things up randomly. I always ask questions when I am trying to understand the Bible. I especially enjoy looking up the meaning of characters' names, because I have learned that names are important to God. All throughout the Bible, the meaning of people's names becomes a pivotal part of their stories. As their stories unfold, we learn how their names are integral to the narrative, foreshadowing life events and often substantiating

Biblical promises.

But mostly, names show us that God has growth, change, and potential for each one of us.

For example, here are some well-known biblical characters who receive a new name from God. Jacob (the supplanter) becomes Israel (the one who wrestles with God). Sarai becomes Sarah. Although both names mean princess, when God changes her name to Sarah, he also adds that she will be the mother of nations, noting a significant new season for her. Saul becomes Paul. Abram becomes Abraham. Simon becomes Peter. The Bible is filled with stories of transformation.

In some instances, a given name describes the situation someone is in or the feelings that have overtaken them. In the book of Ruth, Naomi is a widow who returns to her homeland without her husband and sons and asks people to call her Mara, which means bitter. But despite her request, in the following sentence, she is still called Naomi. Sometimes, we decide what we should be named and God disagrees. Naomi means "pleasant and gentle." Her circumstances were grievous, but those circumstances would change, and she would feel pleasant again.

There is an interesting twist on the meaning of our names found in the story of a character named Jabez. His name means "born in pain." Jabez called upon God to bless him and enlarge his territory. He asked God to increase his impact and influence in the troubled world around him. God granted Jabez this request. In this case, he didn't change Jabez's name, but instead, he changed his future, thus changing the meaning of his name.

Jabez asked God not to let his label be his legacy. God granted his request because he saw Jabez's heart.

What makes his story a little different is that it was Jabez's mother who had the pain when going through childbirth. She was the one who named him, putting her experience over his identity. But the Bible describes him as "more honorable than his brothers." Jabez is often held up as an example of a person who lived a life of faith and trust in God despite his challenges and difficulties. His faith in God allowed him to pray such a big prayer and receive a blessing.

God granted Jabez's request and blessed him with favor, pleased with his honest and humble heart. In this case, God didn't change his name, but he brought from it a new purpose and blessing. Not all sorrow and pain define us. What defines us is our relationship with God.

Do you know what your name means? My given name is Amanda. It has a Latin origin and means "has to be loved." I remember being in middle school when my Latin teacher told me what my name meant. I did not believe in God at that time, but it's dear when I think about having a name standing for love.

Do you know what your name means? You have a unique name. Your talents, interests, and circumstances are all part of what you are here for, and God has a plan for your life. If you're in a place where you feel like you're waiting and unsure what to do, I challenge you to spend some time worshiping God. Ask him questions. Praise him for who he is. Listen for his voice. Write down what he says. Spend time reading his Word. Keep leaning into him expectantly. God will tell you what he has for you to do. It isn't a secret! All you have to do is ask.

After encouraging me with my name, God spoke in a new way. He spoke of a truth which spanned several years of my life. He wrote essential sentences of hope and purpose one word at a time.

Have you ever asked God to give you a word for the new year? I have for years, but the word that he gave me one year was a doozy! The word was vacancy. Who gives someone they care about a word like vacancy?

Chapter Fifteen

Vacancy, an Unexpected Word for the New Year

———————— • O • ————————

Question: If someone told you exactly what you needed to do to succeed, would you try what they said?

————o-o-o————

The word entered my mind like a flower blooming, leaving me silent. As clear as the sound of my voice, I heard it: "Vacancy." The word filled my spirit to the brim. I saw lights, far away at first. The lights blinked in the darkness like city lights. "What is that?" I said, closing my eyes as the lights moved toward me. The vision came into focus, and I could see it was a neon sign blinking in bright red letters, pulsating on and off again, one letter at a time. "V - A - C - A - N -C – Y."

"Vacancy," I exclaimed in utter disbelief. "What kind of word is vacancy, Lord? That is not a positive word for the new year. And why am I seeing a neon sign?"

It was almost the beginning of a fresh new year. For as long as I could remember, I had prayed and asked God to give me a word for the following year. It was more than a habit or a ritual; it was a message and a reminder that I was not alone. I loved doing this because each time, the word God gave me encouraged me and affirmed that he was with me. Asking God for a word reminded me that he knows my future and has already been there. I know he will go with me through every valley and hard place.

My anticipation quickly dissipated. There was no turning back from this moment. I knew it; I had heard the word from God. I smirked, thinking about how he showed it to me this time so I couldn't convince myself I heard him wrong. My days of expectantly wondering about my word and hoping for a word like favor or prosperity were over. I sighed. My word of the year from God was vacancy.

Little did I know that this seemingly negative word was a divine invitation to create a space for God's presence in my life. The word God offered called me to let go of the unnecessary and make room for his purpose. "Vacancy" would catalyze a profound transformation in my life, a transformation I had yet to understand fully.

Standing there, torn and tattered, I offered my new year to God. "Time and life are yours, God; I guess I was asking for things I didn't understand. I lay down my plans, Lord. I want yours." Something shifted in my heart at that moment. I lowered my body to the floor and knelt. "I surrender it all to you," I whispered, feeling a sense of peace and trust wash over me.

I hadn't realized everything I had accumulated over the years. I hadn't only collected tangible things. I had also been managing habits, mindsets, and ways of living that were never meant for me to keep. In this vacancy season, God offered me a chance to start over. He wanted to fill me with more of his purpose and himself, but I had filled my heart, home, relationships, and thoughts with so many things other than him.

Some places looked neat. They were clean and set in order, but there were rooms with piles of clutter covered in cobwebs. Cobwebs are not the same thing as spiderwebs. A cobweb is an abandoned spider web. The sticky silk is meant to catch necessary prey, but it lays dormant and catches dust and debris instead. Under the weight of this unnatural reality, the webs loosen and hang limp in the room's corners.

Picture your heart. Where are your cobwebs? What places have been left so long in disrepair that you have not bothered to clean them, and even the spiders have left because nothing lives there?

God gave me this word right before the world shut down. Only he knew what was coming: the coronavirus pandemic of 2020. In my chaos and uncertainty, God gave me a heavenly glimpse into the good things he was planning to do. During one of the most desolate wilderness times I would endure, God would set the table before me and join me for a meal.

About a week before the world came to a standstill, my son and I moved in to care for my elderly parents. I had a house of my own filled with belongings, and my parents' home was over-flowing.

Looking at all that needed to be sorted and cleaned was overwhelming. "What are you doing, God?" I yelled, but he stayed silent. God had given me a dream to be a writer and a speaker. I had spent years following that pursuit and now this. Every book signing and speaking event was canceled. I couldn't go to church. I couldn't hug my daughter because I went to live with my parents. I wondered what was going to happen to my success. "Was it all for nothing?"

I grabbed the folded piles of clothes from my bed to put them in the black trash bag. "Why bother to be neat?" I couldn't even get moving boxes because of a disease called COVID-19. "This is all stupid," I yelled, after knocking a precarious pile onto the floor. "I give up!" I flopped myself like a rag doll onto my bed.

That is when God spoke. "Embrace the process. Give me your unknowns and trust my knowns. I know the plans I have for you, plans to prosper you and not to harm you, plans to give you a hope and a future."

I lay there silent. I knew those words. God was quoting the Bible. Jeremiah 29:11 was one of my favorites, and he knew it. "That was a brilliant move, God," I said, smiling. "You do know me," I sat up and dusted the dirt from my favorite jeans. "We can do this together," I proclaimed with a new determination.

Like a baby in the womb who floats surrounded by protection, provision, and perfect sustenance, I was encapsulated by his plan. God, who created every system of transformation, knew what stages and changes I would go through. He could see the end result. It takes nine months for a baby to be born into the world. Before that, all the baby knows is God's perfect provision. I pictured a fetus held buoyantly in amniotic fluid, surrounded by safety and silence, fed directly by an umbilical cord. God had created a beautiful universe within the mother's womb.

"Hmmm." I sighed, thinking how beautiful God's plans can be. Being cut off allowed me to view my life from a unique perspective. Maybe I was like a baby in a womb, being cared for ideally by the One who created me. What I didn't expect was the entire world experiencing the vacancy with me.

Something was unnerving about not being able to run to Target when I felt like it. The only places open were my food store and my pharmacy. Amazon and online ordering became my go-to. I hadn't realized how much I went shopping when I didn't need anything until I couldn't go. Growing up, we bought what we needed. Over the years, I learned to shop when I wanted something, instead of pausing and thinking about what I was buying. I went from spending cash to using a credit card. You don't feel the weight of a purchase when you charge it. It isn't until you pay the bill that you feel the weight of your careless spending. I guess that's how I filled my life with so much stuff.

The world and everything in it was changing. I was learning to let go of things I thought I needed. Clinging to anything too hard shrinks the soul. This season was a season for trust and consecration. It was a time for clean, empty spaces for God to pick up and pour through however he saw fit.

My house began to feel much like a cocoon: tight and restricting. But wings are grown in that space. I trusted God to transform me however he saw fit. He wanted me to leave what I had been clinging to and embrace the new experiences he had for me.

Maybe I saw success differently than God did. If I could only embrace the process of his plans for me, I could shift my focus onto his perfection. Embracing the process meant accepting the challenges and changes as part of God's plan and trusting he was leading me toward his perfect will. It was about finding joy in the journey, not just the destination, and understanding that God's timing and methods are always perfect.

It felt eerie inside when I got to my old house to work. The bare walls looked sad and ordinary, quite different from the carefully curated living room I had so lovingly put together. All the furniture was piled in the corner. The energy I had put into making my house feel like a home felt like it was in vain. Plastic trash bags and boxes were scattered across the floor. The place I used to fill with young people from my community group echoed and ached in its current state of emptiness.

Back at my parents' house, I would have to live in one room, making an apartment for myself. It was more like a dorm room than a studio apartment. It would have to serve as my bedroom, living room, and office. Were my days of writing and speaking over? Would life ever seem normal again?

As I tiredly packed my belongings, I realized how much I had that I didn't need. It was a moment of deep reflection on my frivolous living and self-centeredness. The decluttering process became a spiritual journey of removing unnecessary burdens and refocusing on what truly mattered in my life and faith. It was about letting go of material possessions weighing me down and focusing on the intangible blessings of faith, love, and hope.

I fell to my knees in the center of my room, surrounded by piles and piles of things to pack. "Forgive me, Lord," I cried out, lifting my chin towards the ceiling. "I don't need so much of this. Thank you for your patience with me. You have been so kind. Help me, Lord, to be patient with my parents. I am afraid but I know you have asked me to enter this season. I know you are with me."

Tears streamed down my cheeks; trembling, I opened my mouth to sing. "Lord I know you're working; you're working, I trust you are working" The words trailed off as I collapsed onto the floor.

My thoughts went to the world around me. The governor told us to shelter in place. The CDC issued new instructions every day. It became clear that no one knew all the implications of this pandemic.

As I drove from my house to my parents' house to bring carloads of my belongings, it struck me that the towns I went through were once vibrant and bustling, but now they were vacant too.

I ended up throwing away or giving away more than half of

what I owned during the move. God freed me from the need for so much stuff. As I emptied my home, I allowed God to empty my heart too. It was a spring cleaning like no other. Everything unnecessary had to go. I hadn't realized that there wasn't enough room for necessities because of the excess.

In the coming years, God gave me new words like favor, breakthrough, healing, and identity. He reminded me that I was chosen and dearly loved.

God gave me a new platform to share the gospel during my completely cut-off season. I began a podcast from a closet in the home where I cared for my parents. I shared the stories of everyone God brought to me. Together, we shared God's story.

God has taken this podcast worldwide. He has shown me the things I may think are impossible are not impossible for him. He has shown me how all the words he had given me worked together. Vacancy in 2020 made way for favor and breakthrough in 2021, which led to the healing of my identity in 2022. In 2023, God gave me the word chosen.

It was time for a new word and a new year. God's word for me in 2024 was "resurrected." This word means many things, but one thing it meant was that he was resurrecting my dream that I had given him to author a book about people's stories.

The first book I wrote was a compilation of twelve stories. I asked eleven of my friends who had fascinating stories to work on sharing their testimonies. I also shared a part of mine. I gathered them together, put them in order, wrote a beginning and an ending, and created a book. I went through trying to get it published and found that several of the stories had people who had suffered abuse.

The publisher said that I would need to get the abusers themself to sign a release form because of liability, and one of them was deceased. They said, "Then you'd have to obtain a death certificate for them." I remember thinking there's no way I can ask people to do that. I had abusers, and I certainly wouldn't want to do that, so I pulled the project.

I worked on other things, learned I will not compromise what I find essential. The publisher told me that I could have written it in the third person and that they would still take the book, but that took away the story's power, so I put it aside. I never published it, but I kept it, and it was my first attempt at helping people share their stories.

On my podcast, I have been sharing people's stories, and it has been a dynamic version of that first book. When I got the offer to publish this book, I realized God had resurrected that original dream to help people share their stories. This book is an overflow of what I have learned over the past few years, aiding people to share their stories.

God nudged me to start this book while I was working on other writing deadlines. How he miraculously brought it about is another one of those fantastic holy plot twists. It seems God is writing them almost daily in my life. When you take the time to look, you'll see them in your life too. Miracles happen every day.

What if we took the time to shift our perspective and look for God in our everyday moments?

When I learned to trust who God was over whether what he said made sense, I began to receive the blessings he had for me. The heavenly things are like that. We need help understanding things that are not of this world.

How grateful I am for the voice of God that gently leads us step by step along the path he has called us to walk. As we go, he walks with us. Each new gift we open together. We need his Spirit to guide us.

Two steps forward and three steps back seems to be my pattern in life. As much as I want to go where God leads me, I often lose my way. But even when I feel like I'm having a hamster-wheel moment, circling aimlessly, Jesus speaks kind words to me. He encourages my heart and so I can keep going. In the next chapter you will see the heart of Jesus as he encourages me during a difficult time. His love surprises me.

Chapter Sixteen
Meet Me in Galilee

Question: Do you believe God forgives?

———o-o-o———

"No! Not again! What is wrong with me?" I blurted out more loudly than I expected. I didn't want to wake anyone up, and I didn't want anyone to know that I was struggling again. On the outside, I thought I seemed together. I was a writer, a podcaster, and a speaker. I led small groups and mentored young ladies, so why did I still struggle to go to God instead of running headstrong into sinful behavior? We all sin. It's part of our nature, but my first reaction is always shame.

When I sin, I choose something carnal over something holy. When the wrestling in my flesh begins, I can choose to run to God. I could and I should, but I often fail. It is a denial of Jesus' lordship in my life. In those moments, I decide to run the other way from him. Afterward, I feel immediate guilt and shame. I feel weak and wild. I am disappointed in myself, and I'm sure he is too.

Trying to stop sinning is a lot like playing the arcade game Whac-A-Mole. As soon as I win in one area, another one of my weak spots pops up for its turn. It doesn't seem to matter which thing I give in to; what matters is I don't choose Jesus over it. I loaded my Amazon cart with things I didn't need this evening. Scouring the internet for things I want is an easy numbing diversion. Shopping seems safe enough, but when I look for the dopamine release I get when I make a purchase, this momentary pleasure can lead to compulsive shopping.

Whenever I did this, I found myself on a slippery slope. I never went into debt over these purchases, but I noticed a pattern. When I didn't want to work through a complicated emotion or situation, off to the internet I would go. Sometimes, I spent months looking for the perfect antique that would make me happy; other times, I clicked "place order," knowing Amazon could bring my treasure to me the same day. In both cases, once the hunting was complete, I still had those annoying feelings to deal with.

It was easy to convince myself this was healthy, expected behavior, but I knew better than anything that this was a coping mechanism, and just because I wasn't turning to alcohol or drugs didn't make it a good thing. Coping with anger, frustration, and sadness is a regular thing. Trying to alleviate the feelings is not. What is healthy is to sit in my emotions with Jesus. I want to enter the process of naming what I am feeling without judgment and express it in a manner that respects my inner well-being to the safest person I can, Jesus, who died for my opportunity to draw near to him.

I stopped and closed my eyes. After taking a deep breath, I felt God reminding me about a moment when Jesus said to his disciples, "You are all going to deny me, but after I go to the cross, meet me in Galilee." Earlier in that chapter of Matthew, Jesus asked them to stay and keep watch with him in the Garden of Gethsemane as he prayed and worked through the suffering he would do on the cross.

Jesus returned to find his disciples asleep, a poignant reminder of the human condition. The Scripture acknowledges the conflict within us—the spirit is willing, but the flesh is weak. This sentiment resonates deeply as I grapple with my weakness.

Like Peter, we often find ourselves in a predicament. When Jesus forewarned his disciples that they would deny him, Peter vehemently declared, "Not me, Lord. I'll never deny you. I'll die before I ever deny you." I think we've all felt this way at some point, but we cannot keep our promises.

When Jesus tells the disciples to meet him in Galilee, he

talks to me and you too. When Jesus says to us, "I know you're going to deny me. I know you're going to sin. You will fall short; you won't do what you think you'll do. Even so, I'm going to meet with you again. I love you," Jesus is extending his forgiveness and grace.

It brings tears to my eyes, especially right after I have sinned—after I've done what I said I would never do again. I hear Jesus say, "Amanda, meet me in Galilee."

I am sure I would be like Peter too. I am often the one who says, "I'm never going to deny you." But then I do. Jesus gives us grace, the grace we don't deserve, because he loves us. He allows us to tell him we are sorry, to admit we are wrong, and to ask for his forgiveness. Jesus already knew what we were going to do. His forgiveness is not just about wiping our slate clean but transforming our hearts.

In Galilee, Jesus and the disciples did much of their ministry together. It was a place where Jesus had preached, and people had listened. It was where Jesus first met them, where they had been fishers of fish, and he had told them he would make them fishers of men. After Jesus was resurrected, he met them in Galilee.

After Jesus died on the cross, the disciples returned disheartened, defeated, and feeling alone to what they knew before they had met Jesus. They went fishing. From the boat, when they first saw Jesus, they were so focused on what seemed like reality, his death, they didn't allow their hearts room to embrace the actual reality: Jesus is alive! Their disbelief turned to awe when they finally recognized him. This moment is significant as it fills us with wonder, reminding us of the miraculous nature of faith. It shows how faith can transform our disbelief into awe, our fear into courage, and our weakness into strength.

We all have places of regret, but we have a place to go with our regrets because Jesus went to the cross. We have a place to meet with Jesus, who awaits us. Jesus longs to be with us.

When the disciples hadn't caught anything after fishing all night, Jesus yelled to them from the shore, "Cast the net on the other side." A bit stunned by the statement; they paused. What

Jesus said didn't make sense, but when they decided to obey him and cast the net on the other side of the boat, they immediately caught fish—more than they could carry. One hundred and fifty-three fish were in their net.

Having studied this Scripture, I want to share that this stands out because the exact number of fish is used. Instead of saying "a lot of fish," John takes the time to record the exact number. In this narrative found in John 21, the miraculous fish catch is the third appearance of Jesus after his resurrection. The number is intentional, given the lack of precision and detail elsewhere in the story.

According to scholars, the numerical value for the total Hebrew words of one hundred and fifty-three is *Ani Elohim*, which means "I am God." Jesus was declaring his identity and clearly showing them that the way they had become accustomed to catching fish wouldn't work for catching men in the great commission.

Jesus called his disciples to go into all the nations as fishers of men to sinners who need a Savior. Fishing for men is a metaphor for spreading the message of salvation. Just as fishers catch fish, the disciples were to bring people to the knowledge of Jesus Christ, the world's Savior. Instead of catching dead fish, they were to save living people on their way to death.

Another important event in this story happened when Jesus called to the men from the shore as he cooked them breakfast. While they were eating, Jesus asked Peter, "Do you love me more than these?"

"Yes, Lord, you know I love you," Peter replied, saddened by the question.

"Feed my lambs." Jesus looked deeply into Peter's eyes. "Do you love me?"

"Yes, Lord, you know that I love you." Peter's chestnut-brown eyes filled with tears.

"Tend my sheep. Simon, son of John, do you love me?" Jesus asked, using Peter's given name, which made him feel like a stranger.

"Yes, Lord, you know everything, and you know that I love you," Peter said, trying not to weep.

"Feed my sheep," Jesus said one last time. "Truly, I tell you that when you were young, you used to dress and walk wherever you wanted. Still, when you are old, you will stretch out your hands, and another will dress you and carry you where you do not want to go." Jesus said it to show what kind of death Peter would have to glorify God. "Follow Me," Jesus finished with a warm smile, reaching out to put his arm around Peter's shoulder and draw him close.

When Jesus looks at us and says, "I know you're going to deny me. I know you're going to sin. I know you'll do what you thought you would never do, but meet me in Galilee," he welcomes us back into a relationship with him. He will ask us if we love him. "You know I love you," we will answer, echoing Peter's heart. And Jesus will give us our commission to feed his sheep.

Jesus plans for us to engage with others and bring his message of freedom to them. He has asked us to go all over the world. Going is what we are meant to do!

Have you ever thought, "I'm never going to deny you, Lord, not me!" And then, when the time comes, you do? Jesus already knows what we will do. He loves us enough to go to the cross anyway. "Feed my Lambs, tend to my sheep, feed my sheep." Jesus reminds us of the hungry people who have not yet met him.

You can tell your personal story of how Jesus has loved you. The world needs to believe he will do what he says he will do, people need to believe they can trust him, and people need to see the transformation he has made in your heart.

"Meet me in Galilee." What a beautiful thing for Jesus to say! He loves us so much that he would do whatever it took to make a way to meet with us again.

We may have to learn to do things differently, but we must also obey Jesus' plan. We can feed his lambs as an extension of our relationship with him. God is calling us to share our stories of his love. He wants us to remember the times we have had together and all the things he has done.

I have never heard more beautiful words the morning after denying Jesus than when I hear him say, "Meet me in Galilee. I have work for us to do together. I know you love me. Let's do what I came here to do! Won't you help me cast the net of my love over the world? Will you tell them? Will you feed my lambs?"

Inspired by the love Jesus offered me, I have done my earthly best to share it. I know the burdens and wounds my parents grew up with. Jesus was calling me to love them the way he did. In the next chapter I share about my mother's passing and how God bringing me back here to serve my parents was his best plan. The greatest holy plot twist happened during these poignant years.

God somehow pieced together healing and freedom with anger and disillusionment to create a stunning mosaic in my life. Carefully mending me, bonding together sharp and dangerous shards, God created unexpected beauty. In his hands I have been transformed.

Chapter Seventeen

Making Peace with Mom, a New Season with Dad

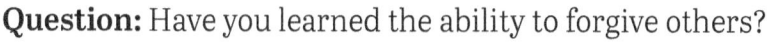

Question: Have you learned the ability to forgive others?

———o-o-o———

Ring. Ring. Ring. The shrill chiming noise woke me from a deep sleep. I sat up in bed and fumbled frantically for my phone. As I reached to grab it from the nightstand, I knocked my water bottle onto the floor. *Thud.* It slammed loudly onto the wide wooden planks and rolled under the bed. "What the ... " I shouted grumpily. The phone was still ringing. "Ugh, seriously?"

I bent down to look under the bed, then remembered to answer my phone. "Hello," I said sharply, wondering who would call me in the middle of the night.

"Amanda," the familiar voice said softly.

"Oh, hi, Dad," I said, changing my tone.

"Amanda, can you come down here for a minute?" Dad's voice was calm, but I could hear a sadness that typically wasn't there.

"Is everything okay?"

"Your mom and I need to talk with you."

"Okay, I will be right there." I slid my feet into my slippers.

Filled with adrenaline, I leaped down the stairs, taking two at a time. I ran to my parents' bedroom. For the four years I had lived with them as their caregiver, they had never called me down in the middle of the night.

The heavy brown door whined loudly as I pushed it open. My

mom was lying on the bed. Her frail hand was holding my dad's hand. He was rubbing the top of her hand and looking lovingly at her. They both turned to look at me. The deep, familiar crackling breath coming from my mom was alarming. I recognized that sound. When I worked with hospice patients, the doctor called it a death rattle.

"Mom." I pushed between them to get closer to her. "How are you doing?" I stammered, trying to keep a straight face.

We had known this day would come. My mom had congestive heart failure, but none of us were ready for her to die. I turned to my dad. "How long has she been breathing like this?"

"For about an hour." His voice was calmer than I had expected.

"She needs to sit up. Her heart is working against gravity." I moved close to mom to sit her up gently. "Dad, get me some pillows." I strained against the dead weight of my mom's body hanging over my shoulder. The weight felt lifeless, like a giant rag doll. Her arms hung limply as I lifted her. "Hurry, please," I shouted, and my dad slid the pillows behind her.

I grabbed my phone out of my pocket to call my son, who was asleep upstairs. "Jackson, I need you to come down to Grandmom and Granddad's room. Right away; it's an emergency." I spoke quickly, then returned to speak with my mother. "Mom, we need to sit you up and clear your lungs a bit."

I looked into her piercing blue eyes. My mother was a beautiful woman. Behind the hurt and pain in those eyes was a kind spirit. Something had happened to her, too, and even though she never told me about it, I could see how she struggled with her emotions. "When Jackson comes down, I am going to build a wall of pillows behind you, okay?"

Mom nodded to show me she understood. "Thank you, dear." Her breaths came short and labored.

"Save your breath, Mom," I said as Jackson approached the door. "Get me those pillows over there, "I shouted, pointing toward the stack of decorative pillows piled in a high tower on the chair by the window. This was the first time I was ever happy that mom had so many pillows. I used to grumble when making her bed in the morning, wondering why anyone needed so many pillows. Jackson and I piled them strategically behind my mom.

"Mom, are you feeling afraid? "I asked her, and she nodded. I reached my hands out toward my son and my father. "Let's pray." We held each other's hands in a circle. Standing there united, I will never forget that moment in time, three generations prayed desperately to God. Jesus entered the room to be with us. I could sense his presence as we took turns praying. The change in the atmosphere was palpable.

After sitting upright for a while, my mom began to breathe easier.

"It's working." I smiled. "Mom, do you feel better at all?"

"Yes," she said loud and clear.

I sighed in relief. "Whew." I wiped the sweat dripping from my forehead. "Thank you, God," I whispered under my breath. I looked out the window and marveled at the starry sky. The light of the moon washed the room in a glow. As it fell on Mom's face, she looked radiant.

When someone has congestive heart failure, their lungs begin to fill with water, and they feel as if they are starting to drown. My mother's breaths were short and sharp. I think that mom would have died that night if we hadn't moved her upright.

My mother was able to get some sleep. In the morning, I got her up and helped her use the commode I had brought downstairs and placed beside her bed.

"I don't want you to have to do this," my mom said sadly.

"I want to help you; I came to help you."

Afterwards, she could stroll with her walker to the table for breakfast. Mom could eat, go to the bathroom, move, and walk on her own. This was her rally day.

The last few days with my mom before she passed away hold a profound significance for me.

Transitioning from a child to a caretaker for my mom and dad had proven to be a journey filled with unexpected triggers and traumas. It required immense courage and resilience to navigate the challenges I faced. It was one of the most difficult times I have ever lived through.

More than twenty years ago, my parents and I discussed my helping them. They wanted to stay in their home instead of going to a retirement facility. But to do so, they would need someone to come and care for them, and they wanted it to be family. At the time, I worked with older people, and I believed I could do it, so I committed to move to their home when they needed me.

Moving back to the home where some of my trauma occurred was not easy. But I knew God was asking me to enter this season.

Admittedly, some moments cut me to the core. There were times when I was trying to do something kind, fun, or new, and my mom, with just one word, would knock everything out of me, like the time I bought a fountain to put outside on the patio. I was so excited to get it set up. I envisioned the days when mom and dad would sit outside and be lulled by the rhythmic tinkling of the water. I planned to surround it with colorful plants and set up two chairs for my parents. Indeed, this would be a happy spot to take them to soak in the sun. But when I went to tell my mom I had bought it, she crushed me with her response.

"Mom, I got this gorgeous fountain." I showed her the picture on my phone. "I want to plant some of your favorite flowers around it, and I already have chairs to set up nearby for you and Dad." I felt so much joy from this little thing. It was something to look forward to during a dismal pandemic season.

"That's pretty," Mom said, looking away from my phone. A look came over her face. A look all too familiar. She was going to squash my joy somehow. I recognized the feeling in my stomach, and my throat felt dry. That is how my body responded to my mom's negativity.

"It's a shame," she said. "Because we have hard water here, the fountain won't last long; it's going to break. You shouldn't have wasted your money, dear." She glared at me. Then she smirked. It turned into a smile. *Why would dashing my efforts make her happy? I thought.*

"Mom, you said you always wanted a fountain. I got this for

you." I walked outside and screamed as loud as I could. "What is wrong with you?" I began to cry. The cycles of interaction always went that way. Just when I thought I could make Mom happy, she found a way to ruin it.

I think she didn't want to get excited about things. It was her self-defense to expect the worst—a layer of anxiety, a need for control, and passive-aggressive tendencies. As an adult, I understood she became this way because of her upbringing. Her childhood had its monster moments too. Perhaps she got a bit of joy from seeing others in turmoil? I will never know why, but it made me feel horrible. Reduced to the frustration and rage of a toddler stuck again in the same toxic relationship scenarios.

But we all grew through these storms and battles. As I consistently served my parents, God worked on my heart. We could never have had the conversations I needed to have if I hadn't lived there. We had to become a team to make it through the pandemic struggles. We even got team hats to symbolize our unity and shared responsibility. We had family meetings about every change and everything that needed to be fixed or reworked. These meetings were a platform for open communication and problem-solving. We did it together.

This caregiving journey produced fruit, growth, and learning. We prioritized the family's needs over our own individual ones, communicated openly and honestly, and worked as a team. This experience inspired hope and resilience, showing us that we could come together and overcome even in the face of adversity. It was a transformation journey, not just for me but for all of us.

I found opportunities to have honest conversations with my parents about things that happened when I was young. I could ask questions, get answers, and get legitimate apologies, something I had never gotten before. These honest conversations and sincere apologies were crucial in healing our family relationships and encouraging and motivating us to move forward.

An apology doesn't change a reality. But it has transformed the things I went through. A sincere apology was more than I had ever gotten before. In some instances, there were explanations.

In others, there never will be, but as I cared for my mom and dad, I healed a little bit more every day.

There were still days when I had to run outside and bite my tongue because I felt triggered. Sometimes, I just needed to walk away because no one understood what I was trying to say or how I felt, and that's okay. I'm a grown woman now and have Jesus to go to. I have a Holy Spirit to counsel me. I have a Father in heaven who knows what's best. My faith was a source of comfort and a guide, reassuring me and bringing peace amid challenges. It helped me find the strength to forgive and heal, and it can do the same for you if you let it.

We talked my mom into ordering a diuretic to help with the water in her lungs. She refused oxygen, and we continued through our day. I persisted in asking that Mom call everybody in the family and have the conversations she needed to have with them, which she did.

I don't know why it was so difficult for her. I don't think she wanted to worry anyone, but I knew it would be essential for those left behind to have a chance to talk with her. The next day the family arrived because they wanted to spend time with mom. By the early afternoon, she was ready to be with Jesus. Mom asked Jesus to take her home.

During the time mom had trouble breathing, I didn't sleep. I was my mom's helper to go to the bathroom, to get cleaned and changed, and to get food. One never envisions feeding their parent, but it was my honor. I had not slept in three days. One of my mom's biggest concerns was wanting to apologize for how things were when I was young. During these moments of helping her with her needs, while we were alone together, she was so honest and earnest.

In her struggle, I found I was finally able to fully forgive her. "I love you, mom. I forgive you. I know you did your best. It has been my privilege to be at the house to help you and dad." I gently rubbed her back.

"Thank you for everything you have done for me," she whispered, putting her hand on my shoulder and drawing me in for a hug.

With the house full of family late Saturday afternoon, I watched my mom's body slump over in her chair. As I ran to catch her, I knew it had been her last breath.

Poof! It was like God pushed a magic button; God moved in my heart, and all the bad feelings were gone. Because of the process of working through the mess of my past with my parents and creating a new present, I was honestly able to forgive.

The memories I have now of my mom are good ones. That's a miracle! I was able to give the eulogy at her funeral. I handled all the arrangements and went to the cemetery to take care of the burial plans. I made picture boards, videos, and everything else that goes into having a memorial service. I paid tribute to the beautiful person my mom was, thankful that I walked as far with her as possible while here on this earth.

It was a journey that blessed me, and somehow, even when I felt something cut deeply, I knew it was because God was doing surgery on my heart. He was cutting memories loose from the places where they had stuck and become strongholds, taking the poisonous parts out and leaving the good.

I wear Mom's necklace every day. When people who know her look at me, they tell me I look just like her, so I guess I wear her smile too. Part of me fully embraces the traumas that my mom went through. I have peace because I know she is no longer anxious and is at peace with Jesus.

Knowing where Mom is, without sin or defect holding her back, is a fantastic balm on my heart. I'm happy for her and grateful that God gave her to me as a mother. I'm thankful he gave me this time with her.

When I look back, I can see those years serving were an extravagant gift. It was what I needed. As I continue to care for my father, we are working our way to the best relationship we can have. We're having many of those healing conversations. Daily, we affirm our love for one another. I am grateful for the earthly parents that my heavenly Father gave me, and I am thankful that they know Jesus.

In the last year of her life, my mother started a new practice that gave me great hope. I retaught mom how to knit to give her something creative to do. Even with her macular degeneration, Mom had the muscle memory to knit again. I got out some of my knitting needles and yarn and sat with her. I would cast the stitches onto the needle and show her how to do it—I got her started by doing a few rows.

Over time, little by little, Mom learned all the steps again. My dad got in on the action the times when the yarn got tangled or my mom dropped a stitch. Somewhere along the way, my mother started the practice of tying a tiny little bow over places where she found a mistake. I love that imagery, looking at our life and seeing a dropped stitch, a missed opportunity, a tiny space, and not trying to hide it, but instead transforming it.

It reminded me of the Japanese practice of golden joinery, an art of repairing broken pottery by mending the areas with gold. Instead of throwing something away as useless, they high-lighted the fractured places, making them even stronger than the original vessel and more beautiful than before. For those of us whom Jesus has transformed, this is his specialty! Our transformations take trauma, brokenness, shame, and regret and turn them into healing, peace, hope, and joy. He continually strengthens those places in captivating ways.

Mom got more enjoyment from creating scarves than anything I've seen in her last years. She must have made a thousand of them. Some went to shelters for unhoused people, some she gave to family members, and some still fill her drawers.

I plan to gather them together and deliver them to a place where people in need can use them. I will also crochet some of them into a colorful pattern with a border and trim to make a blanket that my dad can have as a memory of Mom. In the end, Mom left a legacy of transformation. If she could change at ninety, there is hope for me!

Since Mom's passing, the dynamic between my dad and me has changed. Although dysfunctional places occasionally rear their heads in our relationship, we have settled into a new normal. My dad and I have started a new season.

My dad loves to sit outside in the sizzling summer sun and get a tan. Because my mom couldn't be out on the deck for long, he got his first tan the summer after Mom passed away. I have been able to take my dad out to restaurants again. He can have his friends over to the house for visits, and he gets outside every lovely day we have. I had a palliative care team come in and give him occupational therapy and physical therapy to be sure he was set to go out on adventures. Life has changed.

I always wanted to provide this lifestyle for both of my parents. No one expected a pandemic. After four and a half years of being secluded and restricted, freedom looks good on Dad. I know he misses my mom, but I have kept him busy with good things.

Every morning, when I wake him up, we have a ritual. I go into the room and fill the water for his BiPAP machine. Next, I quietly turn on his light on the bureau. His glasses are always set next to the BiPAP machine and the lamp; I pick them up gingerly and reach toward the edge of the dresser, where his hearing aid is charging. Next, I get his slippers and walker for him to get out of bed safely, and I wake him. "Dad, good morning; it's time to get up," I say sweetly.

"Ahhhh, good morning," he says with a smile. "Thank you for all you do for me. I am so grateful," he always replies.

"It's my pleasure," I respond.

He sits up, puts on his slippers, and stands, pushing his walker towards the breakfast room where I have his breakfast waiting for him, including a steaming fresh cup of coffee. The blueberries, his favorite fruit, sit atop his cereal. His pills and water bottle are right next to his bowl. As Dad sits down, I pour milk into his cereal, and we discuss our plans for the day. Some days, I linger, knowing that any day could be our last.

Dad and I talk about how things will be when he isn't here anymore. He is always purposeful about thanking me for these years of care.

"You took care of me," I say every time.

"Yes, but that was my job as your father. You didn't have to say yes when Mom and I asked you to do this."

"No, but I wanted you to stay in your home together because

this was what you wanted. I am glad I could make this work for you both." We smile with an understanding that there are days when this season is hard for us, but we are bound profoundly and beautifully by passing through it together.

"I love you," Dad says as I leave to do the house chores.

"I love you," I chirp back, meaning it a little more every day. This time has been nothing like I expected, but it was exactly what I needed.

There is something extraordinary about knowing I can love my parents in a way I wish they had loved little me. I know they did the best they could. I used to only say those words, but now I believe them. Every day, I get another chance to serve humbly, talk gently, and help someone in need.

As I grow the fruit of God's Spirit instead of offering a charcuterie of my wounded needs, I can sense God smiling. "Yes, my child, I knew you could do it. Doesn't it feel good to love unconditionally?"

"Yes," I answer, realizing that when I love others as he loves me, I give the love I have been looking for. I want to give it away freely, gladly!

Sweet little me and I have met and ministered to one another many times over these past few years. Perhaps it is why God brought me back home. The day after my mom died, I went out into the front yard alone. The winter sky was resplendent with light. Slowly, I lifted my hands and tilted my head back. Feeling the sun caress my face, I smiled. "Mom, I forgive you," I said, meaning it. "I love you." I started to cry and giggle at the same time. "I will miss you." Then I began to spin. My twirling felt like rejoicing—pure, uncontaminated joy. I knew God was with me. Like a pot thrown back on the potter's wheel, he had been letting me turn. Some of what felt like deep gouges had been his masterful hands reshaping me. He was smoothing the marred places with his perfect work. A potter at the wheel, my life turning in his hands. I trusted him as he was mending me, creating a brand-new creation.

I spun carefree in the same yard I did as a child. Suddenly a snow squall surrounded me. The wind blew my hair gently back and snowflakes began to fill the air. Before I knew it, the ground was blanketed in lily white. "I love you," I shouted with all my might.

In my mind's eye, I saw toddler me standing there, her blonde ringlets pulled tightly into pigtails donned with shiny red bows. She reached out her tiny hands to grab mine. "I love you too," she chirped, and she sang as we turned together in wild circles under the cherry blossom tree. "Ring around the rosie, a pocket full of posies. Ashes, ashes, we all fall down!" At the end of her song, we dropped down to the ground together onto our backs. We spread our arms and legs out wide, pushing them up and down to make magnificent snow angels in the fresh white powder. We were flying. We were free. We had gotten our wings.

I pray that these chapters from my journey have been a door to the amazing blessing of God's presence in a life. And now, it's your turn. Before you begin your journaling experience, I want to talk with you about the impact your story will have in the world.

The next chapter is meant to set the stage for you to begin your journaling journey with God. There is treasure waiting for you. There are sweet and unforgettable blessings coming your way. I am so excited for you!

Chapter Eighteen
Creating a Space

———————— • O • ————————

Question: How does your life impact others?

——————o-o-o——————

As a podcast host, I've discovered the profound joy of intentionally creating a space for Jesus at the table. It's not just about discussing God or his Word. It's about fostering an environment where we can listen to him and engage in a dialogue with him. I've met individuals who are well-versed in the Bible but have yet to experience the sheer delight of sitting with Jesus and hearing his voice.

I included God from the first day I started my podcast. I spent weeks praying and listening for his guidance. After all, the podcast answered my cry to share the gospel, so I needed God to give me the parameters he wanted me to use.

Amid the sea of three million podcasts, mine is a unique space, a sacred haven where I share organically about the God who saved me. It's not just another show about spirituality. I rely on his guidance to navigate this unique journey, and I'm deeply grateful to have you as part of this community.

The interview process begins with a prerecording phone call. During that time, the guest and I become friends. We both share intimately and passionately about our transformations in Christ. There are always things we have in common. There are always things we both learn. After every prerecording call, I walk away encouraged.

The next step takes time. I take the handwritten notes from

our call and read them while asking God to show me more of where his hand was working in my guest's life.

Crafting the questions is crucial for when I will gather with my guests. On the day of the recording, we connect online, prepare, and pray together. As we pray, I welcome God in to be the One who leads our conversation. I thank him for who he is, his plans for this time, and our stories. As I hand the lead over to him and bow to his will for our time together, Jesus sits with us. He is part of our conversation.

My podcast is a sacred space. The time we spend together has no agenda other than sharing the stories God is writing in our lives.

I am penning this book to extend the ministry God entrusted me with through the podcast. My intentions stay unchanged. I aim to prayerfully craft questions that will aid you in spending time with God. If I can create a space for you to commune with God, I am certain he will bless you with his presence. My sole aim is to guide you in creating a space for encountering God's presence and transformation in your life.

Imagine this: You're in a quiet, empty room with this book. You're not alone. Jesus is there, sitting beside you. As you take the time to reflect on your life, he begins to speak. He shares his feelings, reminding you that you heard his voice before you accepted him as your Lord and Savior. His presence fills the room with love and peace, bathing you in his light.

If you take the time to converse with God, I can assure you that he will speak to you. His words carry the transformative power to heal your heart and reshape your life. Remember, God is still penning your story.

My greatest desire is to provide a safe place for you to experience God's love. Before you begin, know I have been prayerful and have spent many hours listening to what God wants me to share. I have no agenda other than to connect you deeply to the One who loves you like no other. My only hope is that you will encounter God's precious presence.

When you invest the time to work through this part of the book, committing to exploring the journaling questions I provide, I can guarantee you will learn things you didn't realize about yourself and about God. You will gain a deeper understanding of your story and begin to overflow with purpose and calling. This is the goal, to help you understand your story, and to connect deeply with God.

Your Story!
Journal Section

———————— • O • ————————

As you embark on this journaling journey, I encourage you to pray each time you write. This practice can help you connect with God and invite his guidance in self-reflection. Your experiences are deeply valuable, no matter how insignificant they may seem. God wants to show you their significance and how they have shaped your spiritual growth.

Here are some journal questions designed to guide you through your self-reflection and spiritual growth journey. These questions are carefully crafted to spark introspection and help you uncover insights about your past experiences, beliefs, and values. Each question will prompt a specific aspect of your life, guiding you to explore and understand how it has influenced your spiritual journey.

Let's begin our self-reflection by delving into your childhood. Our early experiences often lay the foundation for our beliefs and values. Revisiting these formative years can provide a deeper understanding as it allows us to recognize and acknowledge the influences that have shaped our beliefs and values.

Start writing about your childhood. Begin wherever you think you should and share whatever is in your heart. Writing without restraint allows your thoughts and feelings to flow freely onto the page. This process of uninhibited writing can often lead to profound insights and revelations about your spiritual journey. Remember, self-reflection is a journey that requires patience and an open mind. Be kind to yourself and allow the process to unfold naturally.

What was your parents' relationship like if you had a two-parent household?

———o-o-o———

———o-o-o———

If you came from a one-parent household, how did that affect you?

———o-o-o———

Perhaps your caregiving parent was never married; did they date while you were young? And if so, what were those experiences like for you?

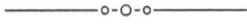

—————o-o-o—————

If you don't have immediate answers to these questions, that's okay. Self-reflection is a gradual process, and it's normal to take time to uncover insights.

—————o-o-o—————

Reflect on your relationships with your siblings if you had any. These connections play a significant role in shaping your past and present and are integral to your journey. Remember, you are not alone in this journey of self-reflection and growth. Your relationships, past and present, are a crucial part of your story.

————o-o-o————

————o-O-o————

Consider your school experience. How did your interactions with peers and teachers influence your beliefs and values? What lessons did you learn about success, failure, and the importance of education? Take a moment to revisit those school days and the lessons they taught you.

————o-o-o————

Did your family, moral compass, or belief system include a religion?

————o-o-o————

————o-o-o————

Reflect on your early beliefs about God. Do you remember feeling his presence or questioning his existence? These experiences can provide insight into your spiritual journey and relationship with God. Take a moment to connect with your past beliefs and how they have shaped your present spiritual journey.

————o-o-o————

Do you ever remember praying or talking to God, being angry at God, or any interaction that started with you?

—————o-o-o—————

—————o-o-o—————

Did you do well in school when you were young? Were you bullied, or did you have a lot of friends and feel confident?

—————o-o-o—————

Was there peace in your family dynamic? Were you able to be who you were? Did you feel loved unconditionally? Or were there conditions in order to feel loved?

————o-o-o————

————o-o-o————

Did you feel like you had to make peace or please people to get along or be popular in school or with your family?

————o-o-o————

Once you got into high school, what kind of things were you doing?

————————o-O-o————————

————————o-O-o————————

If I asked you right now what one memory sticks out from your childhood above all the others, good or bad, what was it?

————————o-O-o————————

In high school, do you remember knowing what you wanted to do in college? Or did you even want to go to college?

———o-o-o———

———o-o-o———

Did you go to college, and if so, what for?

———o-o-o———

Why did you want to do that? Was it your passion or something your parents wanted you to do?

———o-O-o———

———o-O-o———

Was it something that felt safe to do to make a living?

———o-O-o———

What were your friends like when you were a young adult? Did you have faith at that time?

————o-o-o————

————o-o-o————

Many people wrestle with the difference between what their parents believe and what they are beginning to believe at college age. Did that happen to you, and what was the result?

————o-o-o————

Who are some other people in your life that God might have provided to fill a loving role or a role of encouragement? Think of grandparents, neighbors, friends, people from church, and people from school.

—————o-o-o—————

—————o-o-o—————

When did you meet your spouse, if you have or have had one? What were they like? What attracted you to them?

—————o-o-o—————

What was getting married like for you? Did it remind you of your parents' relationship? Was it something you were trying to do differently from your parents, and how did that play out?

—————o-o-o—————

—————o-o-o—————

What was being a mother or father like if you had kids? Were there any undertones of what your mom or dad was like while you were growing up? Did you feel like there were things you were trying to live up to, things you were trying to do differently, or things you were trying to do the same?

—————o-o-o—————

Did your kids go to school, or did you homeschool them? Did you work, or were you a stay-at-home mom or dad?

————o-o-o————

————o-o-o————

If I were to ask you if you had a relationship with Jesus and when you accepted him, do you know when that was?

————o-o-o————

If you know a specific time, date, or experience, write it down and consider why that was the time you gave your heart to him. And if not, consider why you still need to accept Jesus as your Lord and Savior if you haven't yet. Why is that not something that makes sense to you? Would you consider spending time thinking about this?

———o-O-o———

———o-O-o———

What are your thoughts about Jesus? Write them down.

———o-O-o———

Have you ever felt like God was talking to you? Have you ever noticed or heard things in your heart that felt like they came from God, and if so, what were they?

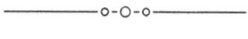

————o-o-o————

What are your talents? What are your passions? Are you doing anything with them? Reflecting on these aspects of yourself can inspire and motivate you to pursue your true calling. Your unique talents and passions are gifts from God and exploring them can lead to a deeper understanding of your purpose.

————o-o-o————

Have you had any significant losses, such as grandparents, friends, or other people who were important to you? Did any of them pass away, and if so, what were your experiences? Maybe the loss was a relationship, a dream, or your innocence. Do you remember what you felt at that time?

————o-o-o————

————o-o-o————

How does your life impact others? What are some things that you do for other people just because it's what you feel you're supposed to do?

————o-o-o————

What are some things you've tried to instill in your children if you have them?

―――――o-o-o―――――

――――o-o-o――――

What are your thoughts and feelings about death and dying? Is it something you're afraid of? Where do you think you go when you die?

――――o-o-o――――

What are you doing right now, whether it's your job or hobby? What is a typical day like, and how is it valuable for you and others?

—————o-o-o—————

—————o-o-o—————

What does the community you're in right now mean to you? How do they support you and encourage you? What difference do they make in your life?

—————o-o-o—————

If I were to ask you what the most important thing about you is, what would it be?

—————o-o-o—————

—————o-o-o—————

If I asked you to share the place you struggle with daily, what would that be?

—————o-o-o—————

If I asked you what hurt you most, what would that be?

————o-o-o————

————o-o-o————

At the intersection of brokenness, trauma, pain, talent, passion, and ability lies your purpose, calling, and reason for being here. You will discover your potential for growth and self-discovery. What do you see that to be? Remember, you are a unique and valuable part of this world with a purpose only you can fulfill.

————o-o-o————

What kind of people are you drawn to care for, pour into, encourage, or advocate for?

———o-O-o———

———o-O-o———

Can you draw an arrow back to why? After doing this exercise, you should see why those are the people you often want to pour into. They're very much who you were as a young person, or they're going through something you've been through.

———o-O-o———

If you could give your younger self any advice, what would it be? Take a moment to reflect on your past, to be reflective and contemplative. What wisdom would you share with the younger you?

—————o-o-o—————

—————o-O-o—————

What do you think is the most important thing you must change?

—————o-o-o—————

Have you tried to make a significant change before? What happened? If you failed, why do you think you did? If you succeeded, why do you think you did?

—————o-o-o—————

—————o-o-o—————

Do you think God might have a good plan for how you could change?

—————o-o-o—————

If someone told you exactly what you needed to do to succeed, would you try what they said?

————o-o-o————

————o-o-o————

What if that suggestion came from God? Would you try it? If not, why?

————o-o-o————

What is a significant loss that you have endured?

———o-o-o———

———o-O-o———

What could you do to make a place of significant loss any better?

———o-o-o———

Have you learned the ability to forgive others? Have you ever needed to be forgiven?

———o-o-o———

———o-o-o———

Do you think forgiveness lets the offender off the hook? Do you believe God forgives? Do you need to forgive God for something?

———o-o-o———

Do you think it's possible to forgive and not forget? What things do you think you can do to find a way to forgive someone who has hurt you? Are you willing to try? Would you be willing to ask God what he thinks about your situation?

————o-o-o————

————o-o-o————

Do you ever notice things that seem out of place?

————o-o-o————

Do you ever wonder why you see them?

—————o-o-o—————

—————o-o-o—————

Have you ever been the only one to see a situation from a different perspective?

—————o-o-o—————

Why do you think you notice the things happening around you?

————o-o-o————

————o-o-o————

Could you believe that these things you notice are God speaking?

————o-o-o————

Have you ever had a job helping others? If not, have any of your employment provided you with opportunities to influence other people's lives positively?

———o-o-o———

———o-o-o———

What did you do with those opportunities? Did you take them? What was the result?

———o-o-o———

How would you define heaven? Do you think everyone goes to heaven? If so, why do you think so?

———o-O-o———

———o-O-o———

Do you believe God can revive the things once dead in your life? Why or why not?

———o-O-o———

Thank you for taking this time to spend with God.
Thank you for listening to his voice and his comfort.
He has great plans for you! I'm excited about this moment
because you have something unique and valuable to share.
Thank you for being who you are.
The world needs you.
God made you on purpose.

– Amanda

Notes

———o-o-o———

Notes

Notes

Notes

Notes

Notes

Notes

Notes

About the Author

· O ·

Amanda Schaefer is a podcast host, author, and speaker. She carries with her the goodness of looking through a lens of gratitude. The *A Cup of Gratitude* podcast is global, reaching over 112 countries and 3000 cities. As a speaker, Amanda teaches the Bible while challenging audiences to live the way God intends. She has a way of making scripture come alive through everyday examples. Amanda's books include, *Crumbled, A Place for Broken People* and *Daily Instaration*. She is a contributing author of *Life Changing Stories* and, *One Chance, One Dance, Don't Miss the Moments in Your Life*, and *Courageous Voices Unlocked*. Her books are down to earth and packed with Biblical truth. Amanda has written articles for *The Brave Women Series, The Uncommon Normal Gratitude Series, The Love Offering, The Warrior Women Series, Butterfly Living, The Empty Nest Mom Series*, and *The Season Series*.

Connect with Amanda at www.acupofgratitude.org or on Social media:

www.instagram.com/acupof_gratitude

www.facebook.com/amanda.f.schaefer

https://youtube.com/@acupofgratitude